A WRITER'S GUIDE TO

OVERCOMING

REJECTION

A PRACTICAL SALES COURSE FOR THE AS YET UNPUBLISHED

EDWARD BAKER

SUMMERSDALE

Summersdale Publishers
46 West Street
Chichester
West Sussex
PO19 1RP
UK

A CIP catalogue record for this book is available from
the British Library.

ISBN 1 84024 010 5

Printed and bound in Great Britain.

Contents

Chapter One

<u>The Author as Salesperson</u>

Do not fall into the error of the artisan who boasts of twenty years in his craft while in fact he has had only one year of experience twenty times.
The Analects Of Confucius

It ain't what you do, it's the way that you do it.
That's what gets results.
Oliver & Young

The Odds Against You

Each and every day, thousands of unsolicited manuscripts land upon the desks of the stressed-out, overheated editors of publishing houses all over the world. And each and every day, those selfsame editors will instruct that thousands of polite "Thanks, but no thanks" letters be sent back to their authors along with the unread material. The reasons given in the standard letter may range from pressure of work to the state of the market, but for the author it doesn't really matter - a rejection is a rejection. And it hurts.

Rejection is a crushing blow to any author. After months, perhaps years, of unpaid labour on a project dear to his or her very soul, the author is greeted not with praise but with a computer-generated letter from someone who can't even be bothered to read what's on offer. Ninety out of a hundred such pieces, in fact, will meet with this fate. The bad news for the would-be author doesn't stop there, either. The odds of those pieces that survive this process getting into print are vanishingly small too. In addition to the above litany of woes, authors face unique problems that are not encountered by any other species of creative artist. A painter, for instance, can hang his or her paintings on a wall and tell the critics go hang themselves! If necessary, it can even be sold on a street corner, where enough people will see it to perhaps start a trend. Likewise, a musician can make direct contact with his or her audience and even cause record companies to sit up and take notice. (Think of punk rock in the late seventies and those who refused to sell it until they saw the money involved.) The hapless author, on the other hand, must seek any audience larger than a gathering via a third party. An author cannot fully function without the permission and help of a publisher.

Faced with these overwhelming problems, many authors simply give up the struggle. The once cherished manuscript that seemed to offer all the promise of a fresh young life is consigned to the attic or cellar. Frustrated and bitter, the author joins the company of those who comfort themselves with the thought that "it's impossible to break in." This is a tragedy in both artistic and human terms. Chances are that the rejected material is no worse than books, poems, plays or films that have "made the grade"; it might even be better in a few cases, and the world is poorer for the loss. It's tragic, too, because of the energy, expense and sheer love involved in creating such a special thing.

That's the bad news. The good news is that it doesn't have to be that way. If you are willing to make certain changes, certain compromises and take certain actions, then a certain measure of success can almost be guaranteed. In the terms of this book, success means one thing and one thing only - publication.

Selling, Not Telling

To tip the odds just a little in your favour you will perhaps need to look at yourself and your work in a very different way. This exercise might offend, annoy or disturb you. Whether or not you are prepared to undergo this process depends upon your desire, your *need* to be published. If your need to be seen or heard outweighs all other consideration then you will get what you want. If not, then the road that you have chosen to walk is going to hurt even more than it needs to. The days when talent, originality and mere genius automatically led to publication are long gone - such traits can even be a disadvantage in a world where everything must be "the same, but different." Novelty is risky, and there are simply too many authors chasing too few publishers for anyone to be able to slip the likes of a "Moby Dick" or "Tom Jones" past the accountants. That's sad, but with very few exceptions that's how it is. Literary output is just a product, and a play, poem, book or film is going to be judged as much by its commercial worth as anything else.

To get published you are going to have to play by the rules of the game. You didn't invent them and you most certainly won't like them, but you are going to have to live with them. This is the first of some very hard truths that you are going to come to realise. The second is that how you sell is even more important than how you write. This doesn't refer to selling to your "public" - that's the easy bit. It means, rather, selling to your first and most crucial reader, the one who can make your dream come true. You must sell and sell hard.

Before you can be read, you must first be bought.

Read the last sentence again and mull it over, because the concept is at the very heart of this book. Unless you can sell your work you are doomed to frustration and despair. This is true whether you aspire to the heights of literary fame or whether you want to be a grubby hack. Without the means to get someone to say that magical "yes", you are never going to have as many readers or viewers as you long for. Forget about composition, style and the things you might have seen elsewhere - you don't need that sort of baggage on this particular journey. Your material is, in the end, less important than your ability to market it. Your writing skills are secondary to your selling skills.

What Gets Published and Why

The truth of this last shocking statement can be proved by visiting any bookshop or watching any television channel. There you will find material so specialised that a dictionary is required to get through the title, let alone the text; there you will find material so crass and rough that it might have been written by a ten-year old who has just discovered naughty words; there you will find material so facile, so mind-numbingly awful that even an insomniac in solitary confinement would think twice about taking it to bed. And yet there it is, staring you full in the face and doing very little good to your blood pressure...

What gets published can sometimes seem obscure, to say the least. *Why* it got published is much easier to explain. The dustiest book on the library shelves has something in common with the bestseller stacked in a pile by the bookshop door:

Somebody was sold it.

That somebody was not necessarily right in his or her judgement, but that somebody did just happen to control the purse strings. He or she was just out shopping, like you are sometimes, and got hooked on an item that simply *had* to be bought. Getting published isn't any more complicated than that - so don't be misled by the mystique that surrounds this job. You do not have to be a genius to get into print. You merely have to give the customer what he or she wants.

Quality and Success

But surely, you will object, shouldn't the quality of my work speak for itself? If I'm any good at all, shouldn't some publisher snatch me up without me having to - blechh - "sell"?

Think about what you've said to yourself there for a moment. The real world isn't like that, is it? Quality by itself does not guarantee success: pick any area of trade you care to mention - cars, furniture, perfume, clothes, insurance - and you will discover that quality is only one of the reasons why a consumer chooses to buy a certain product in preference to others. In a market place jostling with nearly-identical competing brands, other factors come into play, and chief amongst these is sales presentation. We often buy a product that is inferior to a rival brand in quality simply because we prefer its image. The purveyors of such wares accept the limitations of their products and present them in way that will maximise their strengths and minimise their weaknesses. In other words, they sell.

Writing for publication in no way differs from other commercial enterprises, and failure to accept this could cause you some serious problems. By relying on quality alone to achieve your goal you are putting yourself at a grave disadvantage; more than that, you are taking on a very heavy emotional burden. Implicit in this attitude is the feeling that your rejected material must be unpublishable because of its quality. Rather than get into morbid introspection, learn to do what every salesperson does, and *sell* the goods you have available to the best of your ability!

The Numbers Game

Selling is a numbers game. It doesn't matter what you are selling, the principle remains constant and obvious. Make the following your credo, your mission statement:

If I put my work in front of enough people, someone, somewhere will buy it in some shape or form.

Salespeople of every sort quickly learn to honour this golden rule, and so should you. The real secret of overcoming rejection by publishers is, in fact, getting your work in front of enough of them. It's like the lottery: the more entries you have in, the greater your chances of winning. You don't need to be a "top" salesperson to use this system, any more than you need to be a "top" writer. Knock on enough doors and sooner or later you will get lucky. The trick is withstanding the ego-bashing you'll get in the process till the numbers come to your aid.

Setting Sale

By now, perhaps, you might have realised that the aim of this book is to help you reinvent yourself as a salesperson - highly specialised to be sure, but a salesperson nonetheless. Those steeped in the Romantic tradition of Byronic heroes or heroines will, by now, probably be fidgeting as much as the rest of us do when talking about fleas. The whole thing seems tarnished, dirty, because of the lingering afterglow of more innocent times when authors lived off Truth and Beauty.

But it isn't inartistic or unprincipled to work for money or to commission; just think of Da Vinci or Michelangelo any time anyone tells you otherwise. In a way, the situation can be likened to the debate about amateurism and professionalism that has so taxed the world of sport. The existence of professionals alters how amateurs behave whether they will or no; the commercial and competitive nature of modern publishing alters how authors must behave whether they like it or not. If you are writing to please yourself as a form of therapy or self-expression then put down this book at once and read something better. If, on the other hand, you want to get published, then stand by to become a salesperson.

Chapter Two

Planning for Publication

Our plans miscarry because they have no aim. When a man does not know what harbour he is making for, no wind is the right wind.
Seneca

Nothing is more terrible than activity without insight.
Thomas Carlyle

Planning for Publication

A sombre warning that is to be seen or heard in practically every sales office in existence runs something along these lines:

Failure to plan is planning to fail.

This uncompromising message holds true in every walk of life, but nowhere more so than in the world of sales. Plans are vitally important whatever product you are selling, and the lack of them will, more often than not, lead to failure. Without a plan you are rudderless, guideless and friendless, at the mercy of harsh winds that may blow you into emotional reefs, sucking whirlpools of despair. With a plan, however, you have an instrument that can put you back on course if you get lost, one that can steer you safely into port. With the right sort of plan it's almost impossible *not* to sell your product in some shape or form!

A Formula for Success

Salespeople are very fond of unpronounceable words used to hammer home important points. They sound a bit like magic spells and in a sense that is what they are: "Open Sesames" that can unlock the door to success, if used wisely.

One such magic word vital to the planning process is PRAMKU, which states that all goals must be:

Precise
Realistic
Achievable
Meaningful
Known
Understood

The plans that you are going to formulate in order to get published must be exposed to this magical word at every stage. If on doing so they vanish in a puff of smoke, then you know that what you have are not plans but mirages!

Precise means exactly what it says. Stating baldly that you are a "writer" isn't going to help you, your publisher or your agent. You need to establish what sort of writer you are from the word go. If you're writing fiction, is it comic, horror, romance, adventure or what? (Your mind may rebel against such restrictive pigeonholes, but think about the hard-pressed editor who has perhaps fifteen seconds to spare for your proposal. Give him or her a handle to pick you up with - make yourself easy to buy.)

In fact, you must be precise about everything - what you want to write and how much effort and time this will take. Leave the vapours and angst to Victorian aesthetes - this is a job of work that you are about to begin. It may sound more like a time and motion study than Art, but it has its plus side. Imagine how you would feel if, when asked by a friend about your writing, instead of an apologetic mumble, you were able to offer something like this:

"Actually, I've got one project in editorial and another two under consideration." That's not boasting, that's just stating the facts with precision.

Realistic is no less an important word. Your plans may be precise, but are they realistic? If you've never written before and you are expecting to make the bestseller list first time out, then you may be in for something of a disappointment. Perhaps you should "ease" your way into publication via a few less ambitious projects first. Nor should you invest vast amount of energy and spirit on a product that will never sell. Get real!

Your practical goals need to be subject to the same scrutiny. You may "feel" that you can write a book or play in a month as some others have, but is that a realistic goal for you? Judge this not with the eye of an artist but from the perspective of an employee and work within the realms of the possible.

Achievable follows closely on from the above. In all honesty, can you do what you want without making changes to your product? And can you get there with hard work rather than miracles? The precise and realistic goals that you have set need to be achievable within your present circumstances or they will be meaningless.

Measurable is perhaps a strange word to find in a discussion about an "artistic" subject, but it too has its place. You need to be able to quantify what you are doing and have yardsticks that you can judge the quality of your effort by. Be like an athlete or a weightlifter who has definite, but increasing levels of measurable achievement. In your case this might involve target dates for the publication of articles or features leading up to the production of your magnum opus.

Your practical activity must also be measurable. Sections later in this book will show you how to work out how many rejections are required to score a hit, how many proposals must go through to the next stage before publication and so forth. Statistical data can only help you if you know them to be the truth, so learn to measure.

Known means that you are fully aware of the effort required to make your precise, realistic, achievable and measurable dream a reality. You need to know everything involved in the process from the number of tears shed to the postage costs!

Understood means that you, your partner, your friends and your cat realise just what you are letting yourself in for. In some ways you could almost be said to be taking on a new, or second job. You are going to have to stay in a lot, stay up late, buy paper and ribbons instead of luxuries, perhaps. You are going to have lots of "bad days at the office" for sure. Understand in your own heart and mind the changes that this new activity is going to bring. And help those close to you to understand as well, so that they don't feel that they are losing you to an obsession. If that happens they'll end up hating your work, and in the end, so will you.

A Day Out, A Day In
With the PRAMKU formula etched in your brain, you are now in a position to create an effective Action Plan for yourself. All businesses, be they large or small, work to such plans, and so must you. It may seem a million miles removed from why you are writing and what you are writing but it is really, really important that you carry out such an exercise. When did you last set out on a journey without a map or any clear idea of where you were going, how long it would take, and what you would eat in the meanwhile? An Action Plan will give you all of this and more.

Take a day out from your life to take charge of it, to go "inwards" if you like. Leave your work, family or whatever behind for a spell and go to a place where no one will recognise or distract you. A nice hotel lobby is an ideal place to go; you can have refreshments brought when you need them and feel businesslike amid the buzz of the various meetings that will go on there all day. There's no need for you to sit in a garret, there isn't, honestly!

Leave the mobile phone at home if you have one. Should it be absolutely vital then you can ring other people rather than vice versa, but remember that this day is for you and you alone. You'll need writing material, a diary and quite probably a calculator. Get yourself settled and go to work in a relaxed, but thoughtful manner on the first part of this operation.

Taking whatever day that you happen to be planning on as the first day of a new business year, write down your personal and literary ambitions for the next twelve months. Practical ambitions might include things like holidays, buying a car or house. If you can include a few smaller but desirable things as well so much the better. When it comes to your literary goals, both the PRAMKU formula and your reasons for writing (Chapter One) need to be revisited. Your goals and measurements of success must be your own, not anyone else's - how can they be meaningful otherwise? Having carried out the necessary introspection, set down some provisional target dates and stepping stones, i.e. fifty contacts made by the end of month one, a trial article published by month four and so on. (Don't get hung up on the terminology; definitions of these terms will follow after this overview.)

Next, identify and deal with any factors that might impede your productivity. If you need a computer or a new typewriter then make a note of this. Put down any other factors such as the need for extensive research, photographs or the like. Failure to recognise such things can throw your plans seriously out of joint, so be very thorough.

Take your diary and then strike out the weeks and days, when you do *not* intend to work on your product - holidays, birthdays, etc. You won't be able to predict every one, of course, but do your very best. The weeks that you have left in the year after subtracting these will come as something of a shock. That's the entirety of the time that you have available to create, modify and sell your product!

Have a break, not a break-down at this point and go for a stroll, drink or a meal. When you return to work, write up in detail the plans that you have outlined and put dates by everything. Run them through the PRAMKU test again, then sit back and smile. In front of you is a map that is going to take you to the doors of a publisher.

The Sales Week

Whether you are in the fortunate position of having all day to work on your product, or whether you have to cram this in between a job and parenthood, it is essential that you have a disciplined structure to operate within. Working sporadically or whenever you feel like it is about as productive as doing the same at a place of employment. Likewise, if you sit around waiting for "inspiration" you will probably go to your grave unpublished. Sustained, controlled activity isn't romantic, but it does lead to results. Your working week as an author must be as circumscribed as that of any regular employee. It may not be as intensive, but it does need to be as committed and measured. Like most occupations, that of authorship can be broken down into component duties or activities. Believe it or not, in terms of publication writing does not come top of the priority list. Pole position belongs to something else entirely.

Prospecting

A "prospect" is a term that sales professionals use for someone who *could* buy their product but has not yet done so. Looking for such people is called "prospecting" and it is the sales person's most crucial task in any given week. No matter how good a sales person - or writer - you are, unless you have prospects, you are in trouble.

Prospecting is more important than writing if you want to get published.

To achieve a sale in almost any field you don't just need prospects, you need lots of them. Not all prospects turn into clients - in fact the reverse is true. Most prospects will say "No" in a sales situation, that's why supply is such a big issue. A typical customer buying pattern might look like this:

> Ten prospects
> Three sales attempts/presentations
> One sale

The ratios vary from product to product but the underlying principle holds true. Not everyone who sees your product is going to be interested enough to give it serious consideration; not everyone who gives it serious consideration will buy. Most good salespeople learn quickly that the only way to guarantee sales is to contact as many prospects as is humanely possible.

The above principle doesn't mean indiscriminate mass-marketing, however. Prospects need to be "qualified" as to their worth. Qualifying means that you establish whether or not your client has a genuine need for your product as well as the wherewithal to purchase it. There's little point, for instance, in trying to sell coal to a household that has gas powered central heating. Or for that matter trying to sell a thriller to a publisher that specialises in medical textbooks.

Salespeople get their prospects from a variety of sources. In the early stages of a sales career most prospects are "cold", in the sense that they come from directories or business lists. Beyond the fact of their existence and that they might be a potential client, the salesperson knows little or nothing about them. The equivalent for a salesperson who happens to be an author is working through the publications mentioned in Appendix One. Alternatively, you can look at the finished products of publishers or production companies to see if your material would suit their lists.

Later in his or her career, the salesperson will move to working with a different kind of prospect, the referred lead. The referred lead comes from a prospect who has become a client, and who thinks that another prospect might have a requirement for your product. In writing terms this might mean an agent, or a publisher passing your name on to a video production house.

Prospecting for leads of whatever sort needs to become a daily activity in your working week. That's worth repeating and emphasising.

You must look for prospects every working day until you have sold your product.

And then you start selling your next product before the ink is dry on the contract for the first!

Processing Time

Hand in hand with prospecting goes processing. This involves keeping records, chasing up leads that seem to have gone cold, and doing all the humdrum things that help progress a sale. Build time for this essential activity into your working week.

Self-Study Hour

Set aside a minimum of one hour a week to read about writing. Fix yourself a drink, put on some music or do whatever else it takes you to mentally unwind, and then pick up your books. There are dozens of titles to be had on the subject of writing, with new ones coming out all the time. No matter what your medium, genre or need, there is sure to be a book about it. (If there isn't, then write one!)

Even more important than works on technique and style are the sales and motivational texts listed in Appendix One. These may not be as much fun as the outpourings of the great and the good, but they will do infinitely more for your chances of publication.

A self-study hour is a vital part of your working week. In addition to providing you with valuable information, it will also help keep your spirits up. It can even be enjoyable. But do *not* sneak in books that relate to your projects - information on settings, characters, etc. Things like that belong in Research Time; this bit is for you as an author and salesperson, nothing else.

Research Time

Depending on your subject and format, you may spend some time researching your product, accessing photographs and so on. This is necessary and acceptable, but unless you have a signed contract, limit this to work on your proposal and synopsis only. You do not need to be technically brilliant in order to sell your product. You just have to be able to convince your prospect that you know more about the subject involved than he or she does!

Too much information can actually be a bad thing. In sales circles it's commonly said that technical knowledge represents only perhaps fifteen percent of the reason why prospects buy. You need to know that fifteen percent one hundred percent well, however. Ensure that there is enough in your presentation to assure the prospect that he or she is faced with an expert. You can revise anything else before an interview or contract signing; for the present limit your research time to an hour or so and concentrate on *selling*.

Writing Time

Yes, there is something else called writing that you should get involved in. In actual fact, if you are adopting a sales-driven approach to your work there will be very little of this other than sample chapters, tantalisers and synopses (see Chapter Three.) You can write for pleasure as much as you want of course, but if you are writing for publication then you need to be as focused as a laser beam. Your time is too precious to be wasted on churning out products that no one wants. Find out what your prospects lust for and create those instead.

Some authorities recommend that you write every day, but that too depends on why you are writing. Would you work every day for an employer who might not ever pay you, and, if you are to be paid, will pay you fully maybe a year after you have kept your end of the bargain? Trade unions and/or psychiatrists are recommended to those who say "Yes" to this particular question.

A better approach is to do something connected with selling your work almost every day. Almost every day, because a break is necessary to keep yourself fresh and your family free of the suspicion that you have joined a Trappist monastery. Have one day in seven clear of production - and no, that does not contradict what was said about prospecting every day. Send out two prospecting letters the day before instead!

Avoiding Budgetary Burn-out

Emotional burn-out isn't the only kind of burn-out you risk by trying too hard. The business of writing *is* a business, and no business can afford uncontrolled expenditure without facing some very unpleasant consequences. Bankruptcy is unlikely to hit the author (not for this reason anyway!). But it can have nasty side effects. Your partner, for instance, who will already be resentful of lost time, may complain about the amount of hard-earned cash you are "wasting" on your "hobby". Deal with this problem before it arises by fixing yourself a weekly Development Budget.

Decide on a sum of money that you can comfortably afford to spend on your writing each week and learn to operate within it. Postage, envelopes, pens - everything has to come out of this. Squirrel away anything you don't spend and save it for big items like ribbons or paper. Shop around for the best bargains and store discount cards. And remember to keep your receipts against the day when you do start making money.

The above may sound childishly restrictive, but it is a useful exercise, apart from helping to defuse quarrels. Pretty soon your ego is going to take some hard knocks. Your existence, your legitimacy as a writer will be questioned by both others and yourself. The mental infrastructure that you put in such as this will help remind you that you are indeed an author. You wouldn't have these problems otherwise, would you?

Creating a Sales Log

The last thing you need to do in your planning stage is to create a sales log to enable you to record your business activity. You will probably recoil in horror at the thought of bookkeeping rather than book writing, but it is an essential part of any good sales operation. A sales log will enable you to:

- See what you have sent out and when.

- Trace any material that has gone astray.

- Record any comments that might help you modify future proposals.

- Record key contact names.

- Work out the average value of a rejection.

- Work out how many misses it takes to score a hit.

The last two applications of the sales log will be discussed later, but the more mundane uses should not be dismissed out of hand. Pretty soon you will have dozens of letters flying around, some of which will contain valuable information. Most will have all the charm of circulars, but now and then you'll get a comment that can put you on the trail of something good.

A sales log can be established on computer files or in cheap exercise books (one per project). In either case, the log needs to contain the following basic information:

Publisher: it might strike you as unlikely that you would ever forget who you have sent your precious baby off to, but stranger things have happened. Once into the selling mode you will be making lots and lots of contacts, so guard against the possibility of error.

First Contact: call it what you wish, but it is vital to record the date on which you first approached your publisher. Only by monitoring dates can you be sure whether lack of a reply is down to discourtesy or the material having got lost in the post.

Material Sent: just as important is the recording of *what* you sent to the publisher in question. Your proposals, for instance, might evolve to stress different aspects of the topic you are dealing with according to what's in the news. Or again, you might send out an illustrated sales proposal as opposed to a more usual one. Keeping an accurate score will help you determine what works and what doesn't.

Contact Name: you are going to require this for reasons other than courtesy. Most of the larger publishers have quite a few editorial assistants whose onerous duty is to sift through the myriad submissions received each week. You might want to cultivate or avoid this contact later, depending on the sales approach involved.

Response: as mentioned earlier, most of the missives that come your way are going to be valueless in terms of telling you where you are going wrong. Comments such as "does not suit our list" are, on their own, as useless as the "best wishes for placing your work elsewhere" that invariably round off such letters. Just occasionally someone will scribble a more telling remark, however. Treat this information like gold dust, even if it's offensive. There are lots of interesting ways in which you can use such replies when you get into the next stage of the selling process.

Date of Next Contact: more on this in a later chapter. For the present, suffice to say that you are not going to let your prospect go having made only a single attempt to sell it to him or her!
   For example:

Publisher	World Wide Mysteries Ltd
First Contact	7th June
Material Sent	Tantaliser letter A

Contact Name C. Foscoe
Response: Not suitable for their list. Interested
                 in real crime only. (Could I maybe
                 write up source material and send
                 them that? Follow up and give it a try.)
Date of Next Contact: 7th June

Publisher   Way To Go Ltd
First Contact 8th June,1997
Material Sent Tantaliser letter A plus sales proposal
Contact Name S. Cuff
Response: Too busy to look at it.
Date of Next Contact: 8th June

Publisher   Dead Loss Inc.
First Contact 9th June,1997
Material Sent Tantaliser letter A.
Contact Name O. Guy.
Response: Likes the sound of it! Send more
                 details!
Date of Next Contact:

Sales logs should be kept, like business records, for several years after you have sold your material. In the midst of rejections for other projects they will comfort and strengthen, even provide you with reminders of sales principles that you have perhaps forgotten. Who knows, if you write a work of genius, become famous or infamous, they might even be worth money in themselves!

Birth of a Salesperson

Congratulations to those who have suspended their artistic principles, disbelief and outrage to get this far. You now have a vague idea of why you must be a salesperson and how a salesperson operates. There's one final indignity you must be exposed to before you can go into action. Your writing is now going to be turned into a *product*.

Chapter Three

Product Development

Anything that is written to please the author is useless.
Blaise Pascal

We do our best that we know at the moment, and if it doesn't turn out, we modify it.
Franklin Delano Roosevelt

Production Value

Your writing is a product, and in this respect it is no different from tins of beans or soup. Your writing is a product, a purchasable commodity that can be modified according to the needs of the marketplace. Your writing is a product, and you should remember this each time you pick up a pen or sit before a keyboard. Believe and act upon this truth, and you will be published or produced - the laws of supply and demand are going to see to that.

What, then, is a product, and why do people buy one sort of product and ignore another? A product can be defined as a saleable item or service which fulfils the specific need of a prospect. Basic commodities, such as food, work on a fairly elementary level to satisfy hunger or the craving for pleasurable sensations, but some products belong to the realms of dreams as much as reality. The makers of toothpastes, cars and many other things recognise that they are selling dreams: buy this item and you'll be attractive to the opposite sex, your friends will admire you and so on. The product's practical value has become secondary to what it could do for your lifestyle. From now on, learn not to sell books or plays. Sell dreams instead.

The dreams that you are selling in the first instance, however, are not your dreams, they are your prospect's. To obtain a positive outcome, i.e. a sale, you must sell to your prospect's needs, fears and dreams. Identify these correctly and you will be unstoppable, regardless of the quality of your writing or subject.

What Publishers Need...and Fear

Publishers are prospects. Forget about all the self-generated hype and de-mythologise the situation. A prospect is a prospect is a prospect, and they all react in the same way and experience the same feelings when forced to make a decision. The same inner processes work every time. Remember this and refuse to be cowed by the idol that you and others have set up in your mind - it has clay feet.

Why do prospects who are called publishers really buy or reject material? First and foremost, publishers need to make *money*. Lots of other factors come into play, but this need outweighs all the others put together. A publisher needs to be convinced that the product you are offering is saleable to a specified market, that he or she will make "Plenty Much Money" on the deal. Your goal, when it eventually comes to writing proposals, is to leave the prospect rubbing his hands together with glee. You must sell not what's in it for you, but what's in it for the prospect?

The need for *esteem* also figures in the decision-making process. You, perhaps, might enjoy owning fine porcelain, antiques or cars, so that you can bathe in the reflected glory that ownership provides. The satisfaction of having things that other people lust after is immense, and in this respect as in so many others, publishers are no different from other prospects. A stable crowded with big names or unique, quality products is both a source of pride and a lure for yet more winners. At the outset of your career all you can really offer is the suggestion that your product is an essential, 'must-buy' item because of its quality or relevance. Between the lines, suggest to your prospect how good it will feel to own your product.

Fear is an emotion that always skulks in the recesses of every prospect's mind. You're not the only one in a competitive market, you know! A publishing company has to fight hard for its share of the buying public. In that fight, as in any other, costly mistakes can be made. You've heard stories of publishers who rejected bestsellers, classics, fabulous money-earners? Well, so has your prospect! Without blowing your own trumpet *too* hard, stress the opportunity that your product affords and the dangers involved in letting it go. Encourage the fear of missing out that is present in any buying decision, then subtly exploit it.

The Same, But Different

One of the biggest problems faced by an author in any field is the "newness" of his or her product. Despite protests to the contrary, publishers are essentially a conservative lot (and their accountants are even more so!). Experimentation can be expensive, which is why the majority of them plough the same well-worn fields, the ones that have brought good harvests time and time again. At the end of the day, if they could get away with selling the same work under a different title, they probably would. The above isn't possible, of course, even though a look around the bookstores or channels might suggest otherwise. What actually happens instead is that publishers or producers look out for products that are almost identical to ones that have scored already. They want new material to be "the same, but different": e.g., "that series about medical examiners went down well with the punters, can't we have another but with a female lead in a different town?" This attitude may repel you, but it is found all the way through the business, so you'd better get used to the fact. It's terribly stifling of course, and explains why so much which is seen or read is so "formulaic", but it does have its advantages. For those determined to be published at whatever the cost to their artistic soul, it provides useful product specifications. Be "the same but different" if you want to get in print, or else the struggle against the Powers of Darkness will be long and lonely.

There's no escape from this even after publication or production, as the author's work will invariably be likened to another's. Reviews usually say that the author is "another_____" (Fill in your own blanks.) When did you last read a blurb that said the author sounds like him or herself?

Different, But the Same

Of course, if you do exactly what the prospect wants and deliver a near clone, you will at once be accused of unoriginality! This Orwellian "doublethink" is industry-wide, and, once more, there is little point complaining. The only thing you can do is recognise what is going on and try and exploit it. Your efforts, then, must be presented in such a fashion that your product seems to offer a different slant on the subject in question. Whether or not it does or it doesn't is irrelevant; it must *seem* to be different from the others in its field. In tantalisers or proposals you must pay homage to the sales figures of competing works and then proceed to explain why your work will hit the same audience from another angle. You've got perhaps five or ten seconds before the prospect decides that he or she has got one already. Use this time to sell the fact that you have something else, but that your differences are skin, rather than wallet, deep.

Write Advice

An important source of product is actually available from your prospects themselves. Many publishers now offer guidelines for suggestions as to what they want and how they like it presented. Collect as many of these as you can and build up a library, even if at first sight some of them appear to be very different from what you are working on. You have no idea, at the outset of your career, as to what directions your writing is going to take you. The gathering of such material has an emotional, as well as a practical purpose. Receiving such items through the post along with rejections will help convince you that you truly are an author even if you think all looks lost.

Product Diversification

When did you last go in a supermarket that sold only one sort of food? Or, for that matter, a shoe shop that offered only one type of shoe? These admittedly silly examples serve to illustrate a serious business principle, that of product diversity. People who sell for a living invariably offer a range of goods to satisfy every taste and pocket. It's an example you should follow in your writing; by this simple expedient, you can double, treble or even quadruple your chances of making a sale. Variety is the spice of sales life.

Begin expanding your product base with what

management trainers call a "blue sky" exercise. Take a clean sheet of paper and jot down all those things that you have ever fancied writing. Excluding your current project, the one that got you writing in the first place, what really turns you on? Don't rule anything out at this stage - verse, drama, textbooks on worms - just keep the ideas flowing whether they are practicable or not. This, of course, comes next. Go through your suggestions and weigh each up in terms of feasibility, desirability and saleability. Narrow the field of such potential endeavours down to a minimum of four and a maximum of six.

With your products selected, begin to develop them in the usual manner. Research each thoroughly and then draw up a tantaliser, sales proposal, synopsis and sample chapter as part of a package. (See the next chapter for the definitions of these components.)

Developing a handful of products in this way will make you a better writer and a happier salesperson. The improvement in your writing is going to follow on from your hard work and focus; the change in your mood will come about as you realise that you really do have lots of chances of winning!

Your Literary CV

There's more involved in deciding to make a purchase than the merit of the product involved in that decision, however. Today, it is very, very rare for a prospect to go forward without also knowing something of the history of the product and that of the salesperson offering the undoubted "bargain" in question. Think back to when you bought a pension, a car or the house you are living in. Questions about the capability or criminality of the salesperson may have remained unstated, but they doubtless crossed your mind. If you're honest about the situation, you probably bought what was in front of you because of the salesperson as much as the item. People buy people.

Once more, your quarry is no different from any other sort of prospect. A publisher or producer who takes you on is also taking on a big risk in terms of money, time and status. If things go wrong, he or she is going to be the one left with egg on their face. Because of this, publishers quite naturally want to know as much as possible about the person trying to sell them something. They want to know that you can deliver the promised goods, that you have the requisite skills for the job. They want, in effect, a literary CV. The trouble is, if you haven't had anything commissioned as yet, what can you put in it?

Despair not, gentle reader, there are tried and tested stratagems that you can use to sell yourself even if so far you've only written home videos and have never seen your name in print except on final demands!

Before going on to these, however, it's worth considering if you can do the job honestly, i.e., by getting published in a small way first.

Look out for opportunities to get your name attached to something at a local level. Since de-unionisation, it has become much easier for the "amateur" to submit copy, especially if it's at negligible or zero cost. The endless supplements that stuff even the most tawdry of daily rags enclose lots of spaces between the important bits (advertisements) that need filling up. These vacuums provide you with a tremendous opportunity. If your subject allows it, submit a condensed or simplified version with a local "angle." You could also try offering reviews of plays, films or concerts - "mythologise" yourself in your presentation as a man/woman/dog of the people, a veritable Vox Populi. It's unlikely that you'll get paid anything for these efforts, but this is one occasion where you can afford to be generous. Treat such endeavours as "loss leaders", the items that supermarkets give away in order to encourage prospects to buy the items they really want to sell. You are not after money at this stage but something else: credibility.

The next step up from this is to try and get yourself published in a magazine or journal. This is a serious and competitive field of activity, so you may need to consult some of the excellent "How To" books available before going to work. You can again try to sell shortened or simplified versions of a project to general, mainstream publications or, alternatively, you can present work to a more "alternative" market. Out there are some very "out there" publications, and it's perhaps worth trying to use them in your business strategy. To some extent, the more bizarre and obscure your choice is, the better. A prospect may allow him or herself a wry grin on discovering that you have credits in a magazine devoted to Sherlockiana or barbed wire, as well as a few other responses. The fact that you can gain acceptance amongst your peers signals that you write with authority and that you are part of the "scene." Entries like this also give your prospect a great party-piece: "Oh, she was writing for *The Worm Fancier's Journal* before I discovered her." Sell the dream! Prospects *expect* authors to be a little odd, and who are you to disappoint them?

You can always claim to have had articles or items produced of course - but there are real dangers in doing so. Your prospect may call your bluff and ask to see these wondrous creations, in which case you will have no choice but to slink away and hide under a rock. Recovery from such an exposure is almost impossible, so don't try it. Set small, achievable targets and get down to hard work as you prove the truth of the old sales adage: "It's a cinch by the inch and a trial by the mile."

Talk Yourself Up

Another way of filling the credibility gap is to get yourself known as an expert or significant person in your field. This really works best with non-fictional issues where believable facts are accepted even if they are untrue. Nobody wants opinions these days, they want the real stuff. With this in mind, look at your products and see if you can turn any of them into a radio talk or a short lecture. These don't have to be national or to massive fee-paying audiences: small is beautiful just so long as your prospect can see how it relates to your real work.

Don't spend too much energy or time on this option, but on the other hand don't ignore it either. A few appearances on radio, television or the lecture platform will look very impressive on your CV. Your prospect will also warm to the fact that you can obviously present yourself in public and so help with marketing your product at signing, talks and so on.

Economical Truths

If the above steps don't appeal to you, then you're going to have to do things the hard way! With no actual history to present you're going to have to concoct one as best as you can. (It's dangerous to let your product sell on integral strengths without some sort of buttressing. And unnecessary.)

Are you "connected"? Are you a member of any special interest groups that you have identified in your market research? Those who answer in the negative should take out a subscription at once to such organisations and, of course, mention this "inside knowledge" in any submissions. Your prospect doesn't need to know that you joined last week or she will assume that you've been in for years, that you know what you are talking about.

Some salespeople, you might have noticed, are always on the verge of a "big deal". You ought to be grateful, they imply, that they can be bothered with you because next week, well, that's when they are going to hit the jackpot! Salespeople of this sort, are also nearly always dealing with a Mr or Mrs Big, a major company or corporation. The truth in these cases is usually much less glamourous than it is presented. The salesperson may have met with so and so or stepped within the hallowed walls of the boardroom, but as to doing business...? In a sense, though, it doesn't really matter. The salesperson is lent mystique and potency by such associations. A few prospects fall for the line, and if enough do, it ends up becoming a reality.

Being "economical with the truth" is a very weak sales ploy, but if you have nothing better to offer it's perhaps worth a try. Your prospecting activity is going to put you in touch with household names, so why not mention the fact? At any single point the biggest publishers in the world are going to have some of your material "under consideration", aren't they? It might even be "in editorial" - well, that's how you interpret the fact that it's on an editor's desk.

You need to be careful when playing these games lest your flimflam be seen for what it is. Still, a bit of economy never hurt anyone. Ask any politician...

And Your Prospects Are...

The nature of, and need for, prospects - that is, people who might buy your product - was discussed earlier, but it's now time to look at where you can actually find them. More than anything else, the number of prospects that you have will determine your success or failure as a salesperson. Because of this, it is essential that you explore every method of collecting these potential customers open to you, no matter how uncomfortable they may feel. Prospects are what you need to achieve your goal, not talent or style.

The first and most obvious source of prospects are the yearbooks that list them such as the *Writer's Handbook* or the *Writer's and Artist's Yearbook*. These are essential, and should be ordered well in advance of their publication. (Get to your prospect before everyone else does!) Not only do such works provide names and contact numbers, they also include comments on what kind of material is favoured by the companies in question. The *Writer's Handbook* (Macmillan) is especially useful in this context. You can either work through the books as they come or set up separate files, the choice is yours. What matters is that you attack these goldmines as hard and methodically as you can.

You should also be aware of the opportunities contained in overseas directories, some of which are product specific, i.e., lists of companies involved in science fiction or fantasy. Ask at your library or bookshop for such works. The extra posting costs and bother is often outweighed by different attitudes. What fails in the sluggish and conservative British market, for instance, can succeed in the Stateside market. But that's a different issue; for now just concentrate on bulking up your prospect numbers.

Yearbooks have one serious flaw, however. They are annual publications, and sometimes hungry new prospects just appear out of nowhere. Any salesperson will tell you that the best time to catch a prospect is when he or she is just starting up. You normally only have double glazing or a conservatory fitted once, and so timing is crucial in making a sale. As a prospect, you will treat salespeople with interest in your buying phase, disdain when you have the product in question. Prospects who are also publishers have their seasons too. A newcomer to the scene is likely to be less case-hardened, less arrogant. They have a real *need* for material, be it good or bad. At this stage of their evolution, when it's still a dream come true to have packages arrive through the post rather than a fire safety issue, almost every submission will get looked at.

In order to locate prospects at this formative period, supplement your research by reading through trade magazines once a month. Publications like *The Bookseller* allow you to keep your finger on the pulse to some extent. This activity should never replace direct prospecting, of course, but it can be very helpful. For the same reason, if you want to write for television, look at the end credits of programmes that have a "feel" about them that suits your work. Production companies rise and fall faster than publishers, so try and get in early.

There are other specialist magazines worth bearing in mind too. Guild magazines offer valuable information, and sometimes have a small ads section in which agents or new companies will advertise for material. (Avoid publishing companies that advertise in the daily press - these are invariably vanity publishers in another guise.) Computers, too, can have a role to play in prospecting. The internet in particular offers lots of opportunities to reach all sorts of potential clients. Just be careful how you use this amoral genie though - our protection against getting ripped-off is "virtually" nonexistent in cyberspace.

And last but not least, there's good old-fashioned face-to-face prospecting. The different forms of this activity will be discussed in a later section, so for now take it on trust that word of mouth can do you a lot of good. Keep your eyes, ears and mind open and you are going to discover that there are more prospects around than the directories would have you believe.

Alchemy

Product research, whilst laudable, isn't going to excite anyone much by itself. It's raw material, a base metal awaiting transformation into gold, as an alchemist might put it. The magic that is going to turn it into something precious is the subject of the next chapter.

Chapter Four

The Sales Presentation

He's a man out there ridin' on a smile and a shoeshine...a salesman has got to dream, boys.
Arthur Miller

Advertising is the rattling of a stick inside a swill bucket.
George Orwell

—

Art For Art's Sake,
Money For God's Sake.
10cc

The Fine Art of the Sales Presentation

With your action plan complete and your product well and truly defined, you are now in a position to start hawking your goods. This phase of your work is termed the sales presentation and is the most familiar part of the process of buying and selling. It's where you get to light the blue touch paper and retire - literally, if you make a big sale!

For the salesperson who functions as an author, there are two main forms of sales presentation to be considered: one that is conducted through the post and one that is carried out face to face. The former is the most common, but it's as well to be prepared as distinctions often blur. All sales presentations, however, begin with an activity that is also part prospecting, the initial contact with a potential customer. In sales circles it is widely recognised that the decision to buy or not happens in the first ten or twenty seconds of the meeting - the rest is just logical justification of an emotional decision. This principle holds true for the selling of literary products and for whether the sales attempt is made close to hand or at a distance.

First Contact

The first contact that you have with your prospects in this business is usually in the form of written correspondence. Prospects in the plural, note; it's a big mistake to send your material out to one publisher at a time and naively await replies. In doing so you are slowing down an already slow sales process still further and allowing yourself to get demotivated and sullen. Would you sell a house like that, seeing one potential buyer every month? Or would you, rather, announce that it was for sale and get as many people as possible to see it in as short a time as possible? Whichever of the contact approaches listed below you decide to make use of, do lots of them. Be like Mother Nature: broadcast seed as far and wide as you can in the knowledge that perhaps only one has a chance of survival.

What you send out to publishers in order to get a result is largely a matter of personal taste. There are three sorts of "package" you can put in the post, as follows:

(1) A tantaliser or interest-arousing letter
(2) A tantaliser plus sales proposal and a synopsis
(3) A tantaliser, sales proposal, synopsis and a sample chapter or scene

The only thing missing from this list is, of course, the full manuscript. Under no circumstances should you ever send off an unsolicited manuscript - it's bad manners, and bad practice. Once again, put yourself in the shoes of a busy publisher. How sympathetic are you going to be towards a bulky parcel which lands on your desk with a demand that it be read from cover to cover? How sympathetic are you to the junk mail that lands on your mat every morning? (And that's *much* thinner!)

The second reason for not sending off manuscripts until they are asked for is money and energy. Parcelling up reams and reams of paper like this consumes a lot of both these items. Keep hold of your manuscript until it's wanted and show your prospect that you are a professional.

The Tantaliser

At the opposite extreme lies the tantaliser or interest-arousing letter. This is exactly what it sounds like - a brief message designed to provoke a need for more, like the first course or appetiser in a big meal (or indeed, what American TV writers used to call the first scene before the titles in a programme - the Taster).

Tantalisers are commercials of a sort. They are designed to make your prospect want more, but more importantly they are designed to make him mentally "come to you". They are intended to arouse curiosity which will then overcome the natural reaction of a prospect to say "No" to everything. Think of trying to play with a cat. If you reach out, the cat's natural instincts will cause it to back away. If, on the other hand, you look to be doing something interesting, something that's fun and private, the cat will more than likely want to investigate.

The aim of a tantaliser is to excite, not to provide a complete description of your product. Less is more in this case. A tantaliser should occupy no more than a single sheet of A4 paper. Go on any longer than that and you defeat the object of the exercise. Before going on to the actual structure of the tantaliser, it's worth taking a look at some general aspects of presentation that apply to whatever you choose to send off. There is a myth promoted by many "How To Write" books that publishers are not human, leastways not in how they respond to unsolicited material put in front of them. Supposedly, they and they alone do not judge a book by its cover. Viewing material with Olympian detachment, publishers are alleged to be immune to other factors, and consider work presented to them only on the basis of style, quality and merit. This book, however, takes an entirely different perspective. It insists that *publishers are prospects, too,* and like any sort of prospect they respond to certain secondary factors.

As the sales adage goes, "you never get a second chance to make a first impression", so ensure that it is a good one. Put tantalisers on good quality paper with a nice feel to it - try one hundred gramme in a brilliant white. If you are a smoker be careful not to put a negative odour on your material. The smell of stale cigarette smoke is a powerful turn-off to a nonsmoker, and at this stage you have no idea of what your prospect likes or dislikes. Of course, a seasoned professional isn't about to reject the find of the century just because of a pong any more than a prospect is going to reject a find in a junk shop because the owner has bad breath. If, on the other hand, the decision is a more borderline matter, then such things can and do come into play. Eliminate as many possible reasons as you can for your prospect to say "No" and you stand a better chance of getting a "Yes."

The tantaliser begins, as all letters should, with your name, address and telephone number. Next comes the name and address of your prospect. Again, there is more to this than mere etiquette. If you are doing a mass mailshot without a computer, you may be tempted to skip this change to your otherwise standard letter, but this can have dire results. Some editors, perhaps in an effort to suggest that they are hard-boiled Gordon Gecko types, dispense with the social nicety of a proper reply, and send back letters with only "OK, send it" or something similar scrawled atop. Now if you've sent out dozens of tantalisers and all you get back is that and the post mark to go on, you're in deep trouble. (Don't laugh; it happens.)

You have remaining perhaps three or four paragraphs in which to sell your product. Avoiding plunging your prospect into a heavy paragraph that requires a lot of effort to read. Help him or her mentally warm up by offering a brief sentence that sums up what you are trying to sell. An opening sentence for a non-fiction work might read thus:

Dear Mr Prospect,
I am writing to ask if you would look at the proposal for an illustrated non-fiction title, *The Floor Tiles of Monastic Britain.*

This tells your prospect what he or she can expect with a minimum of fuss. The product definition will set your prospect's mind running down well established lines of profit and helps convey a businesslike attitude.

Your next paragraph is in some ways the most important of the entire letter. Essentially, you must condense your entire product and its unique selling points into a few lines. What does it offer, what makes it saleable in a crowded marketplace? Pose a question that only the reading of your full sales proposal can answer and then finish. Tantalise.

Round off with a brief description of who and what you are. Keep this in the third person - an "I" based statement will sound egocentric given what you are going to do next. List any achievements thus far (see

Your Literary CV) and say why you are writing this particular work. Your statements about yourself must be bold, must be in black and white with no greys in between. Think of TV commercials in which everything is bigger, better or new and improved. There's never any "probably" about it, with the singular exception of one highly effective advertising campaign. You cannot go pussyfooting about an exercise of this sort, there isn't the time. If you're an expert in your field, let it be known - if not, be economical with the truth and exaggerate slightly. Whatever image of yourself you are selling, sell it hard. You're an Angry Young Man or Woman with a Cause - get angry. You're an energetic OAP with an interest in writing a keep fit book - go hyperactive. Be bad, be big, but be buyable!

That's all there is to writing a tantaliser. Go to work and experiment until you arrive at something that you like and feel comfortable with. Your tantaliser, along with an SAE for any response, should then be posted out to all the prospects that you have identified. After going through these and achieving no result, write a new tantaliser and start the process over again.

You should, of course, write one tantaliser for each product that you are working on. And you must, whatever else, record the activity in your sales log to avoid approaching the same prospect with different products simultaneously.

The Sales Proposal

As discussed earlier, the tantaliser can be sent out on its own or as part of a package. If used in the first of these ways, a successful approach will lead to a request for further information, and at this point the sales proposal enters the picture. In it, you are going to give the prospect lots of good reasons to buy your product. It has little to do with literature, but everything to do with selling - and getting into print.

As a document, the sales proposal should be between five and seven pages long - anything more will be boring, anything less will make it look as if you haven't given the subject enough thought.

The information that you gathered whilst researching your product needs to be pared down, set down and then jazzed up. But no matter what your subject matter is, *keep it short and simple.*

This applies especially if you are writing a technical work. Just because you know what an LEV or an ADI is, don't assume that your prospect does. His or her readers might, but your prospect is a different kind of animal with different dietary requirements.

The typical sales proposal might contain the following sections, all threaded together to make a persuasive argument:

1 Cover page	5 Structure or contents
2 Introduction	6 Length and delivery date
3 Concept	7 Author details
4 Target market	8 Conclusion
	9 Any appendices

Of course, the above are guidelines rather than something set in stone. You can leave out or add according to fancy just so long as your argument is well presented, and just so long as your length is right. Bear in mind that the sort of thing that you might want as a brochure before purchasing an expensive item that has caught your eye.

To begin at the beginning, a cover page is highly recommended as a way to commence a sales proposal. Once again, the gossipmongers who claim that publishers are above that sort of thing have persuaded everyone that down-dressing is the preferred option. A writer, they argue, should concentrate on his or her writing and leave the fancy stuff alone. Attention to this sort of thing, it is hinted darkly, implies that the author is messing about.

The proponents of the above line would have us believe, once again, that publishers are from a different planet. They don't, it seems, impulse-buy cars, cookers and conservatories like the rest of humanity. They don't, it seems, ever look at pictures of some desirable item and think, "Hey, I want that!". They don't even use attractive covers to sell their own products...or do they?

The simple fact is that visual images can and do sell products. Good covers will not sell a bad book or play, but they can help create buying conditions. What we are creating here is a sales brochure, and how many sales brochure can you think of that don't have some colour, some "life"?

Let's be clear about what's being said here. It is not recommended that you forget writing and go to art school, nor that you should spend a lot of time or money creating images for your cover. If, however, you have used the product design concept mentioned in the previous chapter, or if you or a friend have access to a personal computer, why not use this material to its best advantage? (NB publishers with a visual emphasis or TV and film companies really do pick up on this.)

Whatever your views on the inclusion of artwork, there are some features that a cover page must contain. The most obvious item is the title of your work. This on its own, however, is not going to get across the information that you need to convey in the first vital seconds of the prospect encountering your submission. Underneath your main title, therefore, place a one-sentence summary of the product on offer, e.g.:

Miracles Inc.
An Illustrated History Of The Work Of The St Jude Trust

or:

Another Bloody Sunday

The Proposal For A Three-Part Political Thriller

These are "subtitles" in every sense of the word and show the prospect that you respect his or her time and the rules of the game. The mental effect achieved is comparable to the lowering of the lights before a stage performance. Use your titles to create expectation.

Immediately below these messages should go your name. Space the letters out for a pleasing, harmonious and studied appearance. You are trying to create a mental environment in which the prospect will feel like buying, so seek to control every factor, no matter how inconsequential it may seem.

The eye must then be drawn to a brief list describing the key points or qualities of your work. These are no different really from the product slogans met with in any advertising situation, though you should of course try and avoid the worst excesses of the same! Describing your product too rapturously is bound to lead to disappointment, and in any case will get right up your prospect's nose. Be confident, be factual and infuse your writing not with the qualities that *you* admire but what your *prospect* admires. In this case we are talking about money, target markets, money, glorification of the company and more money. Your prospect wants to be sure that your book is going to do him or her some good, so give the prospect what's wanted in lines that appeal to need and greed. This scene-setting cover page must conclude with your name, address and telephone number.

The second page is a chance for your prospect to draw breath. Outline, in no more than two paragraphs, what your product is and what it is designed to do. Don't get too busy or complicated - this is very much the foreplay stage. If your product lends itself to such, use the first paragraph to pose a question and the second to answer it in a sort of good cop/ bad cop scenario. Interrogate, and ask the prospect to think rather than merely tell.

Keep the whole introduction compact and clean. Let the whiteness of empty space act as a frame to set off your work. Finish with a page number and your name and address. Theoretically, this is meant to save the prospect time and irritation should the pages become detached; practically, this never happens, but doing such once more shows your professionalism.

The page dealing with the concept offers a more reasoned argument for your product. If the introduction was glamour and razzmatazz, the concept is all about showing your prospect how shrewdly commercial you are. Say the same things you've said before but in a slower and more deliberate manner. This does not mean long sentences and technical discussions - the KISS principle still applies, so spoonfeed the prospect with bite-sized chunks. As always, finish off with the page number, your name and address.

When you get to the section marked target market you are really talking the prospect's language. More than almost anything else, this is the bit that matters, the bit that will close the sale. You must reassure your prospect that he or she is not buying a pig in a poke. Using the material brought together in the product development stage, break your target market down in to as many categories as you honestly can. Don't open with the term "general reader", which means nothing at all. Instead, lead off with your best shot, the most focused statement that you can provide. (Detail does not mean length; if you have lots of figures about potential audience size, quote the most powerful and save the rest for a tabulated appendix.)

Your contents section can be quite detailed, an inbuilt synopsis, or a sort of tantaliser for a separate document. (The latter option is to be preferred as it (a) allows you to concentrate on selling, and (b) offers your prospect a chance to take a natural break.) Include in this section, too, comments on structural items such as the number of pictures to be used.

Length and delivery date are two things that any publisher will want to know. Be as accurate as you can with the first - if you are using a computer than a word count of your sample chapter makes this easy; if not, count the words on a page and then multiply this by your projected number of pages. Try to stay middle of the roadish with you estimated size - you can argue about this *after* you've sold the idea!

On delivery date, build in for yourself a safety margin. Work out how long it will realistically take you to get the manuscript or disc ready and then add on four weeks. Should things go more slowly than anticipated you're not letting anyone down. On the other hand, if you deliver early, you'll earn merit marks by demonstrating how professional you are.

The CV that you present ought to be an expanded version of the last paragraph of your tantaliser. Make the most of any "notches on your pen". Even if your work thus far has been unpaid or in minor publications, your prospect is not to know this. If you lack history completely (and you shouldn't if you've read Your Literary CV earlier), then stress the human qualities you have that make you the author for the book or play or whatever.

As to the conclusion, there's an old sales saying that goes, "Tell them what you're going to tell them, tell them, and then tell them what you've told them." The rest of your proposal will have accomplished the first two parts of this process, so concentrate on the big finish. Keep it short and simple, and end again on a question. Try to let your prospect finish the closing thought for him or herself. Make your prospect a partner, not a victim!

Locate in the appendix or appendices any vital information that might otherwise clutter up your sales argument. A good appendix suggests that you know your stuff, so try to include one if you are writing non-fiction.

The sales proposal is now complete. Staple it together or place it in an inexpensive plastic cover - do whatever you prefer to achieve a professional, pleasing look. (Some authorities recommend that staples should be avoided on the grounds that your prospect might want to copy the proposal, but if he or she has reached that stage it won't matter. Concentrate on first impressions and go for a perfect ten out of ten marks for presentation.)

No matter how good a sales proposal is, however, it will still leave out much of the information your prospect needs to make a decision. That's where your synopsis comes in.

Creating a Synopsis

A synopsis can be a product description and a selling aid at one and the same time. If it's a stand-alone item rather than a part of the sales proposal, it should run for between two and three pages at the most. Painful as it is, you are going to have to condense, distil and generally do your work an injustice. Grit your teeth and get on with the job. Summarise only what really makes the product sell and save the rest till you get a contract!

There are a number of different ways to put a synopsis together, all of them equally effective. Your chosen option needs to take account of factors like the nature of your product however, and the level of hype that you've injected into the sales proposal. If the latter has been strong on challenging statements and glitz, then you should perhaps switch gear. Create a synopsis that is stripped to the bone, almost skeletal in its approach. Subheadings within your chapters can be incredibly useful here because they suggest as much as they say. The prospect is able to read whatever he or she wants into these urgent telegraphic messages and virtually sells him or herself in the process! Consider the following summary of Chapter Five of this book, for instance:

Chapter Five: Handling Rejection

Nobody Likes Me, Everybody Hates Me - No Is A Positive Word - The Cash Value of No - Son Of Numbers Game - Second Chances - Backtrack - The Dreams Scrapbook - Your Prizewinning Cheque - Bottled Success - Creating Lucky Streak - Affirmation

Cards - The Hit List - Print, Imprint - Picture This - Look Over Your Shoulder, Mr Publisher - Changing Target - Conclusion.

Fired up by a sales proposal full of suggestions, the average prospect will skip read a synopsis like this and fill in the blanks. He or she is going to be swept along by these tantalising hints of what is in store and will credit you with even more skill than you perhaps have! This is one occasion where you *can* afford to use mysterious "in" words and phrases. You must sell the prospect on the idea that you have got something that he or she needs your help to market.

Another method of presenting your work is to create a synopsis that reads like a story in its own right. This technique is best suited to fiction, where it allows you to really convey the feel of your product. For most authors, describing their work in two or three pages is harder than writing it in the first place; when everything is "essential", what do you leave out? Getting what you want in the length that you need is not easy, and it will perhaps take quite a few attempts to achieve your goal. Keep condensing, simplifying, and then start to put things back in. Quote a few lines from yourself and insert them into the main body of the text. The use of a different type face or colour can make this very dramatic.

Put together your synopsis in the same manner as your sales proposal. Start with a title sheet and ensure that your name and address is at the bottom of each page.

Sample Chapters

In most cases, whenever a publisher asks for further details, he or she will also usually ask for a sample chapter or chapters. These should be readily available from your product design stage and so be familiar, but a few words of caution are appropriate:

(a) Whenever possible, try and avoid sending off the first chapter of a proposed work. Most books or plays take a while to get going and so can be a bit of a yawn in a sales situation. Fiction tends to open with geography or characterisation; factual material generally rehearses the history of the subject covered before offering its unique perspective. Plunge your prospect in at the deep end, though not without a life-jacket. Use a cover sheet to describe the contents thus far and then go into action.

(b) Make sure that your sample is of a reasonable length: i.e., enough to offer a flavour of your product, but not long enough to be intimidating. An acceptance to view your work does not necessarily mean that the prospect is going to buy it. He or she may just be window shopping, so there is no reason in the world why you should waste either your time or his/hers.

(c) Include a number and name on every page, and try to make your sample as free of mistakes as is possible. First impressions count, remember!

An alternative approach to the sample chapter is to create a very busy, action-packed one that really knocks the prospect out. For this powerful, but more demanding technique, see Jute.

Start Selling

All the arrows are now in your quiver; how many you choose to shoot, and in what combination, is a decision for you and you alone. You can achieve results with a tantaliser, tantaliser and sales proposal or the full set. There are no rules as to what you can or cannot do, except this:

You must make one sales attempt every day

A sales attempt, in this definition, consists of the sending out of one letter or package to an identified prospect. You can send out material relating to the same product or alternatively plough and leave fallow different fields, it doesn't matter. What really matters is that you send something out every day in a controlled and sustainable pattern of activity. And each sales attempt, of course, must be recorded in your sales log. After a while, it'll seem very uninspirational and repetitive. Just like a real job at times, in fact.

Chapter Five

Handling Rejection

And he told them a parable, to the effect that they ought always to pray and not lose heart. He said "In a certain city there was a judge who neither feared God nor regarded man; and there was a widow in that city who kept coming to him and saying 'Vindicate me against my adversary.' For a while he refused; but afterwards he said to himself, 'Though I fear neither God nor regard man, yet because this widow bothers me, I will vindicate her, or she will wear me out by her continual coming.'"
Luke 18, 1

Nobody Likes Me, Everybody Hates Me...

So you've analysed your market, identified your prospects and posted the Mother Of All Interest Arousers, having dutifully logged this frenzy in your sales log - what comes next? The short and simple answer, it must be said, is rejection, piles and piles of "Thanks, but no thanks" letters by return post. Occasionally some kind-hearted soul might tell you why your work isn't suitable, but in most cases the replies that you receive will be as anonymous as a bus ticket. The first ten of these you'll greet with a fixed smile and comments to the effect that if it was easy everyone would be doing it. After twenty such missives that smile will be wearing pretty thin, and after another thirty you'll probably be thinking that it's a waste of time, that you were not meant to be a writer, that Fate, her dog and all the capitalist barons are set against you. Stop snivelling. You haven't even started yet.

Rejection letters are not the end of the game but rather the sacrificial pawns, the opening manoeuvres. There are still a great many measures that you can use to make a publisher say "Yes." Before you can do that, however, you need to look at the correct emotional attitudes towards the process in question.

No is a Positive Word

Your practical response to rejection - curl up and die or do something about it - largely depends on the way you feel about the word "No". The analogy of the wine glass that is half-empty or half-full according to the mood of the observer is very appropriate in this context. A "No" from a publisher can raise your self-esteem, help you back on course and even make you money! No is a positive word.

First and foremost, rejection is part of what it is to be a writer; it "goes with the turf" as they say. The very fact that you receive such letters means that you are becoming what you want to be. Rejections are not advertising circulars, nor are they sent out to butchers, bakers or candlestick makers. They are sent out to writers, and in getting them you have something it common with whoever you have decided to make your literary role model. Rejection means that you are an author. Viewed like that, they're nothing to be afraid of, are they?

The second thing to bear in mind is that rejection is a normal and inevitable part of the sales cycle, as discussed in Chapter One. If you were selling insurance, double glazing or cars you would expect people to say no more than they do yes. Writing begins with selling an idea and not everyone is going to like what you've got to offer. To think any differently is to live in a dream world, to be like a boxer who enters the ring never expecting to get hit. Reality will soon disabuse the boxer of this particular erroneous notion, and he will learn to duck, weave and roll with the blows. How to take a good one and come back fighting. Expect to get hit and it won't startle you quite so much.

Thirdly, rejection isn't personal and it isn't a reflection on your worth as a writer. You don't know why, really and truly, a publisher has rejected your proposal. It may be that he or she is snowed under, a previous job has gone wrong, that an argument with a spouse or an overlong lunch is dulling the cognitive faculty somewhat. It might even be that your work is ahead of its time, that no one else has perceived the trend you have spotted. Unless a publisher writes back to say that you are an illiterate twerp, don't try to second guess his or her motives. Just accept the decision and move on to the next phase or prospect.

Fourthly, the fact that you are getting rejections means that you are trying. To receive fifty rejections you must have sent fifty proposals out. Keep that level of activity up and sooner or later you will get lucky. As was said earlier, and as will be said again and again throughout this book, selling is a numbers game. The hurt that you feel is the result of effort, not despair. Dwell on the famous line of body-builders and athletes - "No pain, no gain."

Finally, rejection is a chance to hone your skills. The "No" letters that come through the post can actually show you where you are going wrong. Learn from the experience and make your interest-arousers more punchy, more pithy, more *exciting*. "No" letters can make you a better writer more quickly and cheaply than any correspondence or college course. Those nasty publishers are actually helping you in a strange sort of way.

There's even more to rejection letters than all the above good things, however. Believe it or not, rejections make you money!

The Cash Value of No

Every "No" letter is cash in your pocket. This may sound ridiculous but put aside your preconceptions: for the next few paragraphs you are a salesperson, not an author, and in sales circles it's perfectly normal to calculate the economic worth of a rejection. Here's how and why:

Assume for a moment that the average advance for a first-time, non-fiction author is something around one thousand pounds. Assume also that it takes our starving artist one hundred attempts to sell his or her product. Ninety-nine seeds fall on stony ground but lo, the hundredth takes hold and blossoms. That means that the average value of each letter received back is ten pounds. Isn't that a better way of looking at a "No" letter than a blow in the guts? Rejection, in this light, is just something you experience in order to get what you want.

Son of Numbers Game

Mind-games such as the above are as essential as any practical measures you take in overcoming the effects of rejection. The rest of this chapter is devoted to techniques that you can use to keep your dream alive. As always, they start with a numbers game.

In his classic work *How I Raised Myself From Failure To Success In Selling*, Frank Bettger speaks of an essential quality that the aspiring salesperson must learn to cultivate - "a sense of indifference". By this Bettger is referring not to a lack of energy or enthusiasm for the sales process, but to an almost detached attitude as to its outcome. When a single sale is so crucial that your entire world seems to hang upon it, then of course you are going to be on tenterhooks. A rejection in such a case is going to be as keenly felt as a stab to the heart. Besides which, in a one-shot situation like this your dreams and fears will get there ahead of you. Your prospect will catch the scent of desperation and shy away from you, his or her judgement prejudiced by first impressions. This applies as much to letters and phone calls as it does to face-to-face meetings.

A true sense of indifference stems from one thing only - an unshakeable confidence in your activity levels. If you have only two or three prospects to sell to, then each rejection you receive will come as a crushing blow; if you have two or three hundred prospects to sell your product to, then the situation won't seem quite so grave. You can play the numbers game with indifference knowing that you will win in the end. The moral is don't get mad - get busy.

Bettger's book and its sequel - *How I Multiplied My Income And Happiness In Selling* - are seminal. Read them at least once.

Second Chances

How many attempts to sell to a prospect does the average salesperson make before quitting? The answer to that is a great many more times than the average author makes attempts to sell to a publisher! A salesperson who "died" on a first refusal from a prospect would soon be out of business. He or she will usually make a second, nothing-to-lose pitch. And so should you.

Let's say you've just written a book about industrial pollution caused by multinational companies. The letters went out and, surprise surprise, "Thanks, but no thanks" replies came back. Instead of just taking this on the chin, go into attack mode! Scrutinise newspapers and magazines for items related to your subject, items that

support your case and show that this is a topical issue.
Collect and copy as many of these as you can and then
send them off to the people you've already contacted
once before. Use highlighters or coloured pens to
communicate urgency and slip in a brief note, i.e.:

*Can you really afford to let your competitors get to this story
first? Ann Author, 123 4567.*

Most editors are going to place your second attempt in
that familiar circular filing tray along with the first, but
that doesn't matter. The measure serves to channel
indignation into something more practical and keeps
your all-important activity level on the boil. It also
effectively doubles your prospects - and chances of
winning through - at a stroke. But more importantly
than either of these benefits, it allows your prospect to
have a change of heart. He or she is as beset with worries
about the decision-making process as everyone else and
you should exploit this chink in the corporate armour.
Getting back in front of the prospect will at the very
least show that you are passionate and committed - it
might even get you through to the next stage of the
draw. It doesn't have to work every time. Only once.
You can play even harder - and dirtier - firing off a
third missile. This time, however, send it off not to
your contact but to his or her boss, MD or whatever.

Arrogance of this sort can work at that level - think of the sports stars you just love to hate. You've nothing to lose but a stamp - so attack!

Backtrack

Ideas are like fashions - they come in, go out, come in again. Your play or book or poem might not be the right thing now, but next year who knows? Selling is dependent upon what the market wants, and markets change. Next year, too, that nasty person who said no might have moved jobs. Somebody new will be carrying out his or her role, somebody who might just look at your letter and think "This sounds promising..."

For both the above reasons, make friends with your sales log (Chapter Two). Though it sounds like a boring, bookkeeping rather than book-writing, task, record *every* reply that you get in the appropriate column. A year on, try the company again. And the year after that. You may want to tinker with the title a little or change your interest-arousing letter so that it sounds like a different product even though it isn't. Think of yourself as a trout angler swapping different coloured "flies" around till a fish bites.

The Dreams Scrapbook

The principle of getting a reward for a job well done is ingrained within us from childhood onwards. A sweet from mum, a certificate from teacher, or a word from the boss all serve to reinforce our sense of worth and in so doing spur us on to still greater efforts. With so much going for this important psychological process, it would be shameful not to put it to work for you.

Buy yourself a cheap scrapbook, the kind you might not have owned since you were a youngster. To accompany it make out a list of ten or so reasonably priced treats that you really *want* - a CD, dress, or book, for example. Anything is acceptable just so long as it is well within your financial grasp. This last is crucial because very shortly you are going to start buying yourself these treats.

Scan through magazines and catalogues for pictures of the things that you desire. Keep as close to the image of your original desire as you can; the images must be sharply focused. Cut the pictures out and stick them in your scrapbook, one to a page.

The next step is to link each one of these desirables to a realistic, achievable goal. You might want to link your first treat, for instance, to the sending out of fifty interest-arousing letters. The next could be linked to the first request for sample material and so on. Structure things so that the greater the effort, the greater the reward.

With everything now in place you can start to use your dreams scrapbook. Flick through it as often as you can, especially before going to sleep. Let your mind's eye as well as your physical ones linger over the treats. Imagine yourself owning them, how they will feel, how other people will react to you if you possess them. Keep practising and want them until it hurts. Achievable dreams make wonderful fertiliser for the languishing spirit.

And the minute your goal is achieved, go out and buy yourself that hard-earned reward. Make a note, too, in your scrapbook as to why and when you bought the item. The knowledge that you can hit your stated targets is every bit as valuable as the reward itself and will keep you motivated for much longer.

Your Prizewinning Cheque

An allied technique to the above is that of the prizewinning cheque. Write yourself an undated cheque for a sum that you can afford to spend on yourself as mad money. Link it, once more, to a specific objective and then keep it firmly in sight (on your computer, notebook, etc.). Make sure that you see it and salivate over it every time that you begin work.

On the day that you hit your target, stand up and take a bow - you've just won your first literary prize!

Bottled Success

What's your favourite medium- to high-price tipple? Buy yourself a good quality port, champagne, whisky or whatever somewhere safe. The usual rules apply: the only difference is that if your years of labour come to nought you'll have an investment or a vintage.

Creating a Lucky Streak

All writers, be they working on a poem, a book or a play, dream of a lucky break, the happenstance that will finally see them make the big time. There's no denying it, luck does play a major part in the literary lottery, with the prizes going to the undeserving as often, perhaps, as to the deserving. Luck is essential to your success; the trouble is, by its very definition, luck cannot be controlled. What you can do, however, is make yourself *feel* lucky. In some ways that's as good if not better for your writing.

Start off, as always, at an emotional level before taking any practical steps. Contemplate for a while how very, very fortunate you are to be where you are in this world plagued by famine, war and terror. Your life may not be a bed of roses but compared to the lot of the most of humanity past, present and future it's pretty decent. Though it sounds old fashioned, learn to count your blessings.

On a practical, luck-generating level, do the same thing as you are doing with your writing - get the numbers to work for you. Give yourself a chance to get lucky on the material level. Forget about your dreams of big lottery wins with their weekly expense and their instant demotivation. Enter, instead, free competitions, the kind that you see in papers, magazines or shops. Make it a sort of personal goal to enter at least one of these a day. In a while you'll come to wait for the postman with anticipation rather than dread as all sorts of odd things land on your mat. In amongst that lot, you'll one day find a letter saying "Yes please."

Believe it, do it and it *will* happen!

Those of a superstitious nature could see this technique as using up their "bad luck store" on something trivial. Whatever you make of it, however, it serves as a distraction from the pain you would otherwise feel.

Affirmation Card

These simple but highly effective motivational aids rest upon two time-honoured maxims. The first of these is that "seeing is believing"; the second is that if you say something often enough you'll come to believe it's the truth whether it is or not.

On a sheet of paper write out twenty-one affirmations - that is to say, twenty-one positive, feel-good statements about your writing. These could be lines like "persistence leads to publication" or "I am an author already; all I have to do is get published."

Make the sentences short and as meaningful to your

personal circumstances as you can. Once you are satisfied with the results, type them on to small record cards of your favourite colour. (Try typing the affirmations on white stick-on labels which then carry the aura of official print.) Place one such message on each card. If you are using the Design Focus method outlined elsewhere use a reduced image as a flip-side.

The finished articles should then be placed in a plastic wallet and kept with you constantly. Read through the entire set of cards twenty-one times each day when waiting for trains, meetings, etc. The aim is to have these thoughts percolate down into your positive subconscious where they will drive out negative ones.

The Hit List

According to the controversial studies of an equally controversial psychiatrist, those people who are angry and full of hate tend to outlive their more docile peers. The idea of the grim, obsessive figure is nothing new to fiction, of course, but have you ever thought of using it to write by?

Put together a short letter in which you imagine yourself to be addressing a publisher who has foolishly rejected you. In it, you are going to tell your hapless victim what a big, *big* mistake he or she has made in so doing. You should describe how your book has just made the Top Ten List in the world. How it has just won the Booker, the Nobel, the Pulitzer, and the Best Kept Pet Prize at the village show. How the humble submissions editor who discovered you now heads up an entire division. Pile it high and pile it deep.

For every rejection that you get, put one such message in an envelope waiting to be posted to *that* person. Keep the letters in sight and just think about the pleasure that you are going to get from sending them off.

You don't *have* to send these letters out of course - you can merely use them as a fun motivational technique if you like. But, as the Sicilian proverb goes, revenge is a dish best eaten cold. Enjoy.

Print, Imprint

To return to the subject of rejection letters for a moment, don't throw them out until you've had your wicked way with them. Most rejections that you receive will carry a company logo and then, in bold letters, the name of your submission. Cut these out and paste them in a book somewhere. Your title, appearing in lots and lots of different styles, will take on a certain reality. You're halfway there already - keep going!

Picture This...

Visualisation - creating images of things that you want to happen in order to influence the real world - is a technique used in sport, health and a whole host of other areas. The principle is as old as cave art and as new as pop psychology - any differences are mere window dressing. Two broad categories of visualisation exercise are appropriate to the author suffering from rejection blues. The first type involves picturing a favourable scene in concrete detail - i.e., you might see yourself walking into a bookshop to purchase your published title. For this to really *happen* you need to imagine as meticulously as you can. Feel the pile of the carpet, see people, see your work in the proper section, the proper alphabetical sequence. Keep replaying this motion picture inside your head so that your subconscious gets the message.

The other kind of exercise is a battery-recharging exercise. In this you imagine a calm place or colour, a retreat you can visit in times of stress.

Visualisation is a deeply researched subject with much to commend it. Study the books recommended in the appendix and find out what works for *you*.

Look Over Your Shoulder, Mr Publisher

There is a kind of rejection that is even more painful, even more depressing than the rest, and it goes something like this: "We have read your proposal with interest but we have a very similar project in hand at the moment." This withering reply is perhaps the cruellest blow that can be struck against any author.

The dream of being the first and the best is suddenly seen to turn to ashes as someone else cashes in on *your* idea. They're not even saying you're rubbish this time - they're just saying that you are too late. It's a killing stroke if you stand still and take it, but if you use the principles of the yielding martial arts, you can turn the enemy's strength back against him and convert the rejection into an unusual sales aid.

Actually, what you've received isn't rejection, it's business intelligence of the best kind. Your enemy has just told you in so many ways what his or her plans are for the very near future. Publishers are businesses too, and any business likes to know what its competitors are doing. Knowing is only a couple of steps from doing. Help another publisher steal the march and you can not only see your work in print, you can enjoy a delicious revenge.

Instead of destroying the offending letter take a number of copies. Next, identify your enemy's (the one who rejected you) main competitors by size, style or subject. Write a very, very short summary of your project and explain that it is ready to roll first. Don't labour the point, just tantalise. The subtext your reader picks up will say "if they can make money on this, so can I!". Your effort can ride in the slipstream and get lots of publicity for nothing, or it can act as a spoiler and ruin someone's day. Don't try and guess your prospect's motive - just provide the bullets!

An alternative strategy is to go downmarket or seek a smaller publisher who can score one off the big boys. Or, perhaps, you could consider adapting your work for television, radio, stage or the papers. Whatever you do, do it first! Land the first punch and enjoy the tears it brings!

Changing Targets

If you are consistently hitting a brick wall in your efforts then perhaps you should think in terms of going over or around it instead of through it. What fails as a book might work as an article or TV feature, or a radio feature or a play: what fails as a play might work as a radio feature or a feature or an article...get the picture?

Study the diagram overleaf and from wherever you are on it work your way around. Keep an open mind and experiment. With a little effort you'll be able to come up with many different guises in which your work can appear. Some of them might involve a collaborative effort: e.g., how about your product as a graphic novel or a picture book? Should you lack experience in any particular format then there are plenty of "How-To" guides available. Give it a whirl and see what happens. You could well discover that you've been trying to dance ballet when you're cut out to be a rugby player.

Reinventing your product can pay off handsomely. Aside from getting the thing that's burning inside you downloaded, it will also add weight to your literary CV. After all, if you've had material on television or radio then you must have some sort of "expert" status, mustn't you?

CHANGING TARGETS

BOOK (NON-FICTION)

MAGAZINE / PAPER ARTICLES

FILM SCREENPLAY

TV SCREENPLAY

CHILDREN'S / SIMPLIFIED VERSION

STAGE PLAY

RADIO PLAY

TV FEATURE / PROGRAMME

POEM

RADIO FEATURE / PROGRAMME

BOOK (FICTION)

Same ammunition, different target. Use this virtuous circle to explore new markets and increase productivity by making the most of your research / original ideas

Keep Writing

In the face of constant rejection it is vitally important that you write something every day. You may want to defenestrate the computer, hire hitmen or take up budgie breeding instead, but you must resist the temptation and continue to work. The projects that you have established can be your best tonic in this situation. If project one isn't moving then go on to two or three or four so that you are constantly fresh. Write for the love of it for a while again. It's a little like sex: you can enjoy it lots without producing a baby every time!

Keep Reading

In the depths of despair you should also pay special attention to your self-study hour as described earlier. Avoid the smug outpourings of those who have done it in "How To" books; these will only make you feel more wretched. Look up the motivational texts listed in the appendix instead, and concentrate on fixing your emotions rather than any imagined fault in technique.

Conclusion

The methods outlined above *can* and *do* work - if you let them, that is. You must, must, *must* guard yourself against the erosive effects of rejection and use every trick in the book to overcome it, no matter how wacky or strange. And you must also keep sending interest-arousing letters and proposals out. Think numbers.

Of course all this is working on the assumption that everyone has said no. What happens when they say yes is the subject of the next chapter.

Chapter Six

Sales Meetings

A Spartan, on going to war, complained to his mother that his sword was rather too short. "Then get one step nearer," she said.
Plutarch

Pressure people with what they desire in order to sound them out, and the inner correspondence will inevitably respond.
The Master Of Demon Valley

Yes, But...

The moment when a publisher actually gives you a provisional "Yes" is going to be both exciting and terrifying. Exciting needs no further comment, but there are several reasons why such good news can throw you into a panic. It's the big break, the chance that you've been waiting for all these years. And it might go wrong.

Put the above mingled emotions on hold for a while and continue with your sales work. Until you have a signed contract in your possession you have absolutely nothing. You are still in a selling situation and any relaxation on your part may cost you dear. Should your prospect change his or her mind, should economic circumstances alter, you will be gutted by this last minute failure. Continue to send out proposals - if another publisher says yes then you can compare the deals on offer. Besides, won't it be nice to say no to one of them? Don't celebrate till you have a contract.

An acceptance may come to you through the post in the form of a letter of intent and a contract. Quite often, these may be several months apart - your prospect may need to have meetings with colleagues, banks, etc. Take this at face value and, as discussed above, carry on prospecting during the interval.

Whether or not you choose to accept the first contract offered depends entirely on whether your need to be published outweighs your avarice. There are no right or wrong responses to this situation, it's a matter of how you feel. From a practical standpoint, however, you must ensure that if you're not getting the best deal, at least you won't be horrendously short-changed. Most publishers are honest, but at the same time they are also in business. What's good for them or their company is not necessarily the best for you. Before you sign on the proverbial dotted line, check the contract through carefully. Consult some of the excellent writer's books available on this specialist field, call your guild or try and interest an agent. As the proud possessor of an unsigned contract, you are a different proposition from most of the hopefuls that contact such organisations day in and day out. The ten percent or so involved could be more than justified by your new-found friend picking up on something you hadn't noticed. Give it some thought, especially if you're the sort of person who never reads the small print until it's too late.

Nice to See You?

Between a publisher expressing an interest in your work and the actual signing of contracts, there may also be another stage. The prospect may suggest a face to face meeting in his or her office to chat things over. Once more, control your natural delight and recognise this for what it is - a sales opportunity. A sales opportunity for which you need to be well prepared.

A face to face selling presentation that is unplanned nearly always ends in failure or worse, a desire to "think about it." You cannot just go into sales mode at the push of a button, and least not without some considerable experience or skill. Something vital or significant will get lost in the heat of the moment, and your prospect will leave the meeting still undecided. Preparation and planning is essential to get the result that you want. The truth is that a good sales presentation of this sort should be as well scripted as a stage play where the lines of one character are immediately met by a response from another. You need to know, as producer of this drama, not only all the words that the characters will be speaking, but the emotions they will be feeling as well. This may sound fanciful, but it isn't. A sales presentation follows rules as rigorous as any Greek tragedy or Elizabethan sonnet. If you see a sales person give a "natural" performance, then check carefully and you will find that he or she is using a format that use has made as comfortable as a pair of slippers. Even things like the changing of pens, the taking off of spectacles or gestures are scripted. Read some sales books and then think back to the last time you were sold anything...

A face to face meeting with a prospect has a number of distinct phases which, though they often blur in practice, can be defined as follows:

(1) Icebreaking
(2) Presentation
(3) Trial close
(4) Close

All of these elements have a place in making the perfect sale happen. Miss one out and you may have to retrace your steps or even argue your case, and that is the last thing in the world that you want to be doing in this situation!

Warning: Thin Ice

To repeat a maxim stated earlier, you never get a second chance to make a good impression. The emotions generated in the first few seconds of any contact between two human beings linger on through whatever else follows to colour expectations and create outcomes. Because of this, you must take your "stage entrance" very, very seriously. As with most performances, the action begins long before the curtain rises - in make-up, in fact.

Make-up

What are you going to look like on your Big Day? This isn't as silly a question as it sounds, because that will influence the way that your prospect behaves towards you. Are you going to look like what you are supposed to be (Angry Young Man, Designer Icon, etc.), or like somebody the prospect can talk "business" with? If the first, then you might want to exaggerate your qualities to sell your image; if the second, go conservative and respectable. (It's always better to assume the second persona will be required unless your research tells you otherwise.)

Treat the whole exercise like a sort of date. Your prospect has to fall in love with you a little, so pay attention to details. Get your hair done and take a toilet kit with you for grooming just before "going on." Carry some perfume or aftershave, along with tooth brush and breath freshener. If you're a smoker, *don't!* Avoid cigarette smoke beforehand and don't light up unless your prospect offers to do so first.

Looking sharp has additional benefits besides reassuring your prospect. As the expression goes, if you look good, you'll feel good. The added confidence that this part of your preparations will bring is going to come in useful when you actually start to sell.

Timing

A peripheral item often ignored by even those who should know better is arriving at your prospect's workplace or home exactly on time. A prospect can be late if he or she chooses, but a salesperson cannot. This may seem unfair; tough. Any delay is going to rankle your prospect ever so slightly despite goodnatured protests to the contrary. Don't start your meeting by having to apologise. If you are travelling from a distance, make sure that you are fully aware of your route and add thirty minutes to your E.T.A to be on the safe side. Should you arrive early, don't just blunder in. Observe correct business etiquette and keep to the schedule. You can always use the spare time to polish your lines!

Action!

The icebreaking proper begins the moment you walk through your prospect's door. In a publishing house of any size, you will usually be asked to take a seat; unless you are going to be kept waiting for some length of time, avoid this. Stay on your feet so that you can greet the prospect as an equal. The body language is all important here (see below). A physical ascendency leads to a mental one, so don't put yourself at a disadvantage. The publisher is *your* prospect, even though it may seem the other way around. If you don't control the situation your prospect will.

On this last, you may find your wait going on a bit longer than anticipated. This may be genuine, or it may be a ploy to gain an edge. Assume the latter just in case, and staunchly refuse any offers of tea or coffee. Accepting refreshments is almost a magical formula invoking your presence as a prospect. You'll suddenly be forced to smile and apologise as you splutter a mouthful of something somewhere. Keep loose and ready for action.

At some point during the day, you will be invited in to the prospect's office or lair. Watch for signals as to whether the prospect wants to shake hands - not everyone likes to make physical contact before a deal, so respond accordingly. As you are invited to take your seat, there will probably be some aimless chitchat along with a mental clearing of the decks. Smile at your prospect and sit down in an unhurried fashion. Relax, or at least pretend to!

Louder than Words:
A Brief Digression on Body Language

During this ice-breaking phase, your prospect will be forming his or her first impression of you. Consciously or unconsciously, the prospect will be picking up physical signals that may or may not be compatible with what you are saying. Despite our boasts and technologies, we human beings are still animals and share the responses of all other mammals to pleasing or worrying situations. Blushing with shame, flushing with rage or paling with fear are only the most obvious of these reactions. We are constantly transmitting unspoken messages, a fact known and exploited by salespeople of every ilk.

Body language, to give kinetics its more popular name, is something that has captured the public's imagination of late. Nowadays, very few management types are unaware of its ramifications and uses. This can be seen in everything from office layout to interpersonal behaviour and dress. To get the most out of body language you should really do some serious reading on the subject, but here are a few general things that you can watch out for in yourself and others.

If you are wearing a jacket, try to unbutton it before you sit. As to more formal presentations that require you to use, say, a flip chart, take it off altogether. Why? The reason may sound bizarre, but it shows that you are not carrying weapons (a hangover from other times, one would hope) and that you are confident enough not to need any "armour." Try and watch topnotch trainers in action. Very few of them keep their jackets on longer than the first fifteen seconds of impression-making.

So far as sitting down is concerned, try to angle your chair so that you are more or less on the same "side" as your prospect. You can't climb over the desk, but you can position yourself so that you are in a less confrontational situation. Later, when you do your presentation, you can slide around to point things out in the proposal.

Try to avoid "leg locked" or "arms crossed" postures, which can indicate unfriendliness or worry. By the same token, note these in your prospect. If the conversation stagnates and you see this fixed attitude, try and prize the armour loose, e.g. "You look a bit tensed up, Ms Prospect, is there something wrong?" Most people will become very self-conscious and this point and will open out, simultaneously removing the mental blocks they've erected. Or they might just tell you if you have said something upsetting. Either way, you need to know.

Be watchful for mouth-touching gestures linked to conversational assurances in others, and wary of it in yourself. We are told from childhood that lies are bad, and all but the most accomplished liars give away clues when challenged. Should someone be giving you lots of reassurances but constantly shading or covering their mouth, then you might be getting fobbed off.

The movement of the eyes in relation to questions can also give you valuable hints about what your prospect is feeling and even his or her psychological type. Knowing this, you can change your vocabulary to utilise words that will have the most effect.

There is also a technique called "mirroring" that you can employ when dealing with prospects. As the word implies, this involves copying certain postures or gestures in order to indicate shared feelings, a commonality of interests. You've probably seen this process at work many times without particularly noticing it. Next time you're in a public place, watch people engaged in serious conversation. More often than not you will see them leaning forward or planting chins in palms as if they were indeed reflections. Or, perhaps more aptly, two puppets pulled by the same strings. There's nothing new about this phenomenon; the ancient Malaysians, for instance, observed many centuries ago that when you think of a person you take on some of his or her physical habits. The only difference with the modern version is that it is used to control or influence. Initially, the person wanting to "take over" might mimic the prospect in order to get on the right wavelength. He or she would then take the lead. As the prospect begins to mirror, his or her mind and emotions begin to move in the direction required.

There are those who would say that the techniques outlined above have nothing to do with literature or art, and in this they are absolutely correct. Such methods *do* belong in the world of sales, however, and this is the world you are intending to conquer. Those readers less squeamish about using such ploys in order to sell their work are advised to consult Robbins and Pease (see Appendix).

Present and Correct

It's most unlikely that your prospect has invited you to his or her office to study your body language skills, however. The fact that you have been requested to visit means that your prospect is seriously interested in your product but that he or she may have a few reservations. You need to encourage one set of feelings and eliminate the others. This you can do by means of an effective sales presentation.

Have with you copies of your sales proposal and synopsis. Your prospect will probably have his or hers too, possibly with a few notes on them. This is where your correct chair positioning will pay off - it's easier to read from the side than from upside down for most people! If you can sneak a quick glance at what the possible worries might be, you can steal a march and show how thoughtful you are.

You should also have a nice pen with you. Not a chewed, part-digested cheap model, but the best that you can manage. This is your magician's wand, a tool that you can use for controlling your prospect's attention. He or she will follow the pointer, and follow *you* if you do it properly.

Run through your proposal briefly, but don't make this a sermon, your prospect must feel that he or she is being worked with, rather than worked on. Don't narrate; ask your prospect questions that will help you towards your goal. Try to collect lots of little "yes" responses that will add up like a ton of feathers in your prospect's mind (i.e. did you like the artwork, the length, etc.). In any sales situation, when a prospect gets used to saying yes, he or she is more than likely to say the same when it gets to the big question. At that point, lean back, smile and wait for feedback. Your prospect may then reveal what is bothering him or her, or what else is required. When this happens DO NOT ARGUE OR CORRECT. Buy yourself time with phrases like "I see what you mean" so that you can give a considered response. Move around the desk, if you're not there already, and use your pen to add or delete. And keep asking questions. Let the prospect tell you what he or she wants exactly.

Into the conversation, you should also be weaving what are called "trial closes". You can't just say to a prospect "Do you want it or not?" - a question like that stands a fifty per cent chance of rejection. Look to offer, instead, either/or options, for instance, "Would the shorter version or the extended version be better for you?" Trial closes are like the feints and jabs of a boxer that set the opponent up for the knockout blow. Use two or three at least of these - really good salespeople may make up to as many as eight or nine in a presentation. And they get results.

You are now coming to the big finish, the close. The result that you want is a yes or a no; a "maybe", or "think about it" response is worse than useless. It wastes everyone's time and will frustrate you more than an actual rejection. If things have gone swimmingly, then you can move to the next phase of negotiations without further ado; if not, then you have some work to do. Sometimes your prospect will tell you directly what the problem is, in which case all you need do is compromise and deliver. A situation that is more difficult to handle is when your prospect says that he or she will "let you know." Don't get irate when this happens; use strategy instead. Look defeated and let your prospect believe that the matter is closed. If you're wearing glasses, this is a good point to take them off so that you look even more naked and defenceless.

You need now to discover what the hidden objection really is. Go through, quietly, all the things that your prospect did like. Again, ask, don't tell. Build up the reasons for saying yes once more and then give it your best shot. If your prospect tells you what the real snag is, ask if he or she will sign if that is put right. If the answer is in the negative, look for another prospect.

Advance Guard

One reason why a publisher might want to see you is to discuss the size of any advance. An advance is just what it sounds like, a sum of money forwarded to you in anticipation of the profits that your product will generate. This is generally payable in three instalments, one on signing, one on delivery of your product, and one on publication. Any company person worth his or her salt is going to try and keep the figures involved as small as possible. There's nothing personal in this - it's just business. Be businesslike yourself. If you go in low you'll come out lower, so start with a higher figure and allow yourself to be "beaten" down. That way you both win.

Not all companies offer advances. You should try and stick to ones that will, but there are occasions when you may have to compromise and wait for royalties instead, i.e. if no one else wants the product. Accept this in the knowledge that you have achieved publication, and in the knowledge that you will do better next time.

Chapter Seven

Work in Progress

Production is not the application of tools to materials, but logic to work.

Peter Drucker

It is not enough to be busy...the question is, what are we busy about?

Henry David Thoreau.

Carry On Selling

The sales process is a bit like painting the Forth Bridge - by the time that you've reached the end, the first bit needs painting again. Or to put it another way, it's like the seed that is planted, grows, flowers and produces more seed. Break any part of that sequence and you have death, not life.

You cannot, *cannot* afford to stop selling if you want to continue being a published or produced writer. No matter what deadlines you face, what your current prospect wants and when, you must ensure that your proposal for something new goes out every day. Bear in mind that it takes the average project around two years to go from idea to production stage. Concentrate exclusively on work in hand and you will suddenly find yourself in a "dead spot" as you wait on someone else making a decision. You'll have to do it all again quite needlessly.

You need to carry on selling. Fortunately, this time there are certain ways of cheating.

Same Again Please

You've just broken into Fort Knox, The Holy Of Holies, The Temple Of Doom - are you really going to be content with just that? Of course you are not! Your prospect is about to become a client and really wants you to think him or her a nice person. Your prospect is still in buying mode so while he or she is still smiling encourage another positive decision.

Sell your second product at the same time as the first.

Think it over - there must be some unfinished business you can turn into a saleable item. If you're writing fiction, how about a prequel or a sequel, spin off adventures of characters that only had bit parts. If you're writing non-fiction, what about the material that you couldn't fit in to your first work? (You could even deliberately stint and aim at a double-whammy, but this has its own dangers.)

An alternative strategy works best with large publishers, who have lots of divisions. As you "decide" whether or not to sign, ask for a personal introduction to the fiction/non-fiction department or wherever it is that you want to go next. Make it a sort of unstated emotional condition for your prospect to do this and your progress through the ranks will be both smoother and swifter. You have nothing to lose and everything to gain, so ask!

Write The Same Book Twice
Well almost! This principle follows directly on from the last, and works just as well with plays and screenplays as books, with non-fiction as well as fiction. Let's say

you've written a book about alternative energy sources. All the painstaking research that you've done is still fresh in your mind, so why not put it to good use? You could quite easily turn it into a young person's book by leaving a few things out, putting a few things in. Or again, let's say you've written a book on motivational techniques for salespeople. The selfsame techniques could, with a little tinkering with the vocabulary, be applied to nurses, teachers, club leaders, directors...

The advantages of plagiarising (sorry, adapting) your own work are considerable. For starters, it will remove any lingering fear you might have that you are a "one hit wonder." Secondly, it will allow you access to new, unexpected markets and encourage you to explore. And, last but not least, it will make you some money!

You can also use this as a honey-pot to lure an agent. The fact that you have had one work published or produced could be accidental; with a calculated second work in hand you are starting to look like dinner. Strike the right note of confidence and humility and you could well ensnare this elusive creature.

Carry On Selling II

Any salesperson will tell you that the best time to make a sale is right after you've just made one. In such a situation you will feel that you are "on a roll", that you can conquer the world before tea. Use that momentum to good effect and try to market your products even more urgently. Carry on selling!

Selling Yourself

Once you are published or produced, then you yourself will also become a saleable product. People will pay for your time, opinions or knowledge whereas beforehand they would probably have rejected you. If you have hit the big time, then your agent will doubtless help you make the most of this sales opportunity; if not, and you are operating at a less exalted level, read on.

The act of publication carries with it a sort of "expert" status, one that can be exploited to good advantage. Not only will this earn you extra income, it will also raise your profile and encourage sales. It even gives you the chance to sell to your clients directly!

How you sell yourself in practice depends to some extent on your literary product, but there are a number of common features involved. Begin by looking out for arts or literary festivals where you could perhaps function as a speaker. As a "local" you can enlist all sorts of help from libraries to councils. Should your product lend itself to straightforward exposition or tuition then your performance content is a simple matter. Just use slides, pictures or demonstrations to give it a live action quality. If your product is fiction-based or otherwise different, then take a "how it was done" approach. Stress your trials and troubles or go into the mechanics - if you have written a crime story or a play, for instance, you can talk about plot devices and the like.

Schools, colleges or specialist societies can also be useful fields to plough. The spin-off of this sort of work is that it allows you to make lots of useful contacts who might help your career in ways you can't even guess at yet. Any such talks must, of course, feature a slot where you peddle your wares. Most publishers allow the author to buy in bulk copies of his or her work at a reduced rate, which you can then sell on at just under cover price. (When you are doing this be careful not to give *too* much away during your presentation. Leave the audience hungry for more and hint darkly at the things in the book you can't talk about.) Newspapers, radio and local television should not be ignored either. All of these are hungry for copy, and even if you don't manage to arrange payment the exposure will boost sales.

The above may seem a long, long way from where you came in, but don't dismiss it out of hand. There are many writers active today whose talent for self-publicity is at least the equal of their artistic talents. If you want to write for a living rather than a hobby then you should investigate this sort of performance art.

Enrol in a drama group or on a public speaking course
if necessary and get into a position where you can sell
in as many ways as possible!

Son of Writing for Money

There is said to be, hopefully metaphorically, more than
one way of skinning a cat; there is, most certainly, more
than one way of getting paid for your literary
endeavours. Quite a few organisations now offer
financial support to authors in the form of grants or
bursaries, and you should not leave these out of your
plans. They invariably have strings attached, but they
are still worth investigating. Read through directories
such as *The Writer's Handbook* and measure yourself against
the stated requirements of each funding body. Obtain
further guidelines from those that seem appropriate to
your circumstances, and then begin a sales campaign
exactly as you would if seeking a publisher. Quantify
and magnify your problems and needs, stress your
potential and above all sell yourself as a worthwhile
product that requires a kick-start.

There's also a way in which you can offer your product
for free and still make a living from your authorship.
You can square this particular circle by making use of
something that has invaded almost every area of human
activity - sponsorship. Money is always available for
projects that serve a worthy cause, and with a little

imagination you can turn yourself into one. You can use your gifts to satisfy your own inner needs and enrich the lives of others - and get paid for it too!

To obtain the kind of funding that you'll require you must first have a definable, quantifiable goal. Perhaps you might want to use your skills to turn fragile oral history into a more tangible record; perhaps you might want to use writing as a tool for helping the maladjusted or disadvantaged to come to terms with their experiences of the world. Whatever it is you want to do, you must be *precise*. (Go back to the PRAMKU formula in fact!) Specify the groups you want to do things with and put numbers to them, together with geographical boundaries. Sponsors of good causes are no different from publishers insofar as they want to see their investment well spent.

With your project defined, spend some time researching your target market. Enlist the help of relevant support, neighbourhood or pressure groups, who will in all likelihood help to fine-tune your proposals. Keep them away from the selling of the proposal to a possible sponsor, however; that's your job.

Turn your findings into a brief selling document, the kind you would send to a publisher. Use the KISS principle - Keep It Short and Simple. Once again, the kind of person that you are dealing with is not going to have the time to wade through massive tomes. Besides, these are boring. Think of kindling a fire, and how too much fuel can smother a vital but uncertain flame.

Start with a bullet-point front sheet explaining what your project is, who it's for and who you are. You should then follow on with the relevant sections as in a normal sales proposal but with one significant addition - a budget. At this stage include only an overall cost and a few general areas of expenditure - save anything more detailed for an appendix. Your budget must include everything from materials to the hire of premises and, of course, a fee for yourself.

Once you have a concise and costed proposal, you can then begin to sell it. The exact nature of your project will to some extent determine what sort of sponsor you should approach, but there are three main categories you ought to consider for almost every submission:

Business
Both large and small companies can be useful sources of funds. Not only can your project earn them praise for artistic, highbrow concerns, it can also offer them a chance to show their sympathy for the needs of the local community. You will, of course, give them full credit in the media for their innovating aid.

Government Agencies
This category includes local, as well as national bodies. Although the former are not as liberal as they used to

be, there is still room for well argued proposals of a short term nature, i.e. a summer-long writing project for disadvantaged young people that could steer them away from the boredom-induced vandalism that costs councils a lot more money than you are quoting.

Central government is even more subject to the whims and moods of the time than the above. Some of the organisations you approach will have constantly shifting goalposts and a structure worthy of Kafka, but persist. The rewards can be considerable for you and those you choose to help.

Trust funds

Believe it or not, there are actually organisations that enjoy giving money away. There are literally hundreds of trust funds in existence whose sole purpose in life is to help projects such as yours! Go to your local reference library and consult works such as *The Directory of Grant Making Trusts*, which will tell you who gives what and why. After that, it's just like finding a publisher! It's a numbers game too, so start sending lots of proposals out until you get a yes.

All the above, by the way, is not intended as an alternative to writing, but an extension of it. Between advances and royalties you need to maximise your income from as many possible sources as you can. Your publisher is not going to look after you once he or she or it has your manuscript, so make sure that you do!

On Literary Competitions

A few words on the subject of literary competitions; enter them at your own peril! This may sound to be in flat contradiction to what was said earlier about the need to diversify, but in sales terms not all business is good business. Business that will demotivate you or business that has to be bought is nothing but fool's gold. Literary competitions can fall into this category. They may seem to be a short cut to fame and fortune, but in reality they are beset with problems. Consider the following:

(a) The chances of your work getting selected by a panel of judges from amongst the thousands of others submitted is no greater than that of selection by an "unfriendly" publisher. The only difference is that a publisher will do more for you.

(b) Rejection in the form of not winning a competition is much more depressing than a "no" from a publisher or a producer. In the latter case you can always tell yourself those "necessary lies" - that publishers are philistines, that great works are often rejected and so on. Failure in a competition for new authors is another thing altogether. You have been judged by your peers and found wanting. There are enough problems out there to demotivate you already. You most certainly do *not* need a more personal rejection that will really hurt.

(c) Many competitions ask for an entry or registration fee out of which the few prizes on offer are paid. This is going to double or treble your business costs and eat into your development budget (Chapter Three). To go back to the lottery example quoted earlier, would you buy a ticket three times more expensive than the rest which offers a lower chance of winning a smaller prize? I didn't think so?

(d) Perhaps the most crippling effect of a failed competition entry is the belief that somehow you have had your idea "stolen". Send your manuscript to a publisher and as like as not it will be read by someone with the soul of an accountant. Send your manuscript off to a literary competition, however, and it will be read by judges who themselves might be writers. They are not going to plagiarise your work directly, of course. It's just that all those ideas that didn't take wing are going to hibernate in the minds of readers until, one fine day, they emerge as some dazzling butterfly that's the same as yours but different. Maybe the author of this successful piece read the same obscure medieval manuscript as yourself, maybe heard the same odd story - it happens. But if it happens to you following a competition entry you'll never be able to shake the outrage, bitterness and pain it brings. Never.

Literary prizes are a different matter altogether. These can be both prestigious and lucrative, but because they are usually awarded *after* publication, there are no dangers attached to them. You will face stiff competition, but make sure that either you or your publisher complete the entry forms for those you are eligible to enter. As seasoned "comperes" say, you've got to be in to win!

Co-Authorship

An option that you might want to consider if the wells of inspiration run dry (or indeed, as a "way in" to publication), is working with a saleable name or talent. Co-authorship is especially useful in instances where one party has the "gift of the gab" but nothing much to say, and the other has a lot to say but lacks the ability to get it down. Like any good sale, this should be a win/win situation where each partner stands to gain.

Products such as those outlined above are both surprisingly common and popular - do a brief count the next time you visit a bookshop! In actual fact, a bookshop is where your research should begin. Leaf through a few such works in different fields and see how they read. In most cases you'll find them informal, chatty and not too difficult to write. First, however, you must catch your expert!

Draw up a list of the "great and the good", the weird and the wonderful that border upon your particular circle of humanity. List anyone and everyone at this stage without regard to quality or feasibility. The one-legged window cleaner at Number 46, the bus driver who moonlights as a guinea-pig trainer, the local tattooed lady, all of these and more should be considered. You may not at first be able to think of such a singular individual, but don't be discouraged. In today's interconnected society we are very much closer to each other than we would like to think - or admit. Ask your friends or workmates for a referral to someone with an unusual talent or history. Follow these up and then ask them for their contacts. As the ripples spread out you will discover some amazing connections. Keep asking and prepare to be astonished!

Once you have decided upon a few really good prospects, do some general reading on his or her subject if appropriate. Skip read enough to be able to hold an informed conversation - you're not the expert, but on the other hand you need to be able to laugh in the right places. Be on the lookout for saleable ways of presenting your prospect - "idiot's" guides, updated editions, illustrated editions, etc.

With all this under your belt, you can start to sell yourself. Send a letter, make a phone call, or even better get a personal introduction to your prospect. Set up a meeting and sell. The last word is very important. You are not there for edifying conversation, vanity or fun, you are there to create a product. As often as not you will discover that your prospect has been "meaning to write a book" for ages, but never got round to it. Fine. You are going to give him or her the opportunity on a plate. Take notes, drop hints concerning your knowledge of the world of publishing, drop titles but above all *sell*.

If your expert agrees to play, draft up a simple contract or agreement. Canvas opinions and ideas as to where other books in the field are going wrong (these will usually be forthcoming). Gather this information up and put together a proposal that gives your expert the glamour treatment, with you modestly bathing in reflected glory. Be like the salesperson who sells the quality of his or her company. Keep a sales log and keep your collaborator informed. And don't forget to stress all the hard work that you are doing!

The advantage of co-authorship is that it will enable you to tackle subjects that you might otherwise never have even thought of. Your partner's expert status can open doors that would have otherwise remained closed, and the exercise can bring you both money and status. Not that it's all a bed of roses - there are dangers inherent in this approach, such as arguments over who does what and when. These practical difficulties should not deter you from what can be a very, very useful sales technique.

On the Books
Now that you have proven yourself as an author, let others know about it. Register yourself with "packagers" and video production companies, who might at some stage in the future invite you to do some work for them. A "this pen for hire" approach can help generate extra income, which in turn will allow you to work on the stuff that really matters. It will also do wonders for your literary CV.

Carry on Selling III
When you sell something it's perfectly natural and proper to want to celebrate. Amidst your jubilation, however, you must also continue to prospect for new work. Be like the snooker player or chess player who is always working several moves in advance. Failure to continue prospecting will result in what salespeople term a "boom and bust cycle." Your writing life will become a series of peaks and troughs, and the troughs will feel all the deeper because of your previous "high." You'll think you've "lost it" when in actual fact you've merely ignored a basic sales law. Don't give yourself the chance to get flattened by rejection again. Carry on selling.

Chapter Eight

Rejected Revisted

By perseverance, the snail reached the ark.
Charles Haddon Spurgeon

From the errors of others, a wise man corrects his own.
Publilius Syrus

Rejection Revisted

And now for the bad news. The last chapter was but a pleasing fantasy and you haven't sold a bean, never mind a book or a script! There isn't a cheque in the post, publishers are not duelling at dawn for the rights to your work, and the rejections are falling with the persistence of rain during an English summer. How does that make you feel?

You'll want to quit if you're honest about it. You've been hurt and the hurt keeps on coming. If you didn't feel some pain and despair following on this you'd be dead. But to quit, to stop *being* what everything in your gut tells you that you are, is that really an option? Can you cease from an activity that's as essential, as natural as breathing, just because you've had a few setbacks?

Giving up is a heavy price to pay for a little hurt pride and an unnecessary one at that. All you need to do is learn how to sell and it's no big deal. Once upon a time you discovered how to walk. You stood, fell, cried, stood again until you eventually walked. Once upon a time, you looked at strange, indecipherable symbols on a page, turned them into sound and then back in to words again. You have already done much, much harder things in your life than get published! Remember that when the despair sets in, and learn to smile through your tears. Getting published is a learning process and sometimes that process hurts.

Keep Your Distance

Your work is not you: it's a product. And that means when people reject your work they are only rejecting a thing. If that thing isn't working, why should you expect them to buy it? Would you knowingly buy a broken washer, lawn mower or TV set?

Put some emotional distance between yourself and your product. Make it something external and you'll be better able to cope with its inadequacies and failings. When your car breaks down or your plumbing fails do you sit down and weep, or do you take practical measures to fix it or get it fixed?

Not selling your work is just a practical problem, and you can handle that if you really try.

Judgement Day

Counting your rejections as a sign of failure indicates that you still do not fully understand the sales process. It indicates that you are judging yourself on the basis of effort rather than the *outcome*. The outcome, whether it's the case of Robert The Bruce's spider getting where it wanted to be or Edison inventing the light bulb on his one thousandth attempt, is the thing that should really be your measure. Edison, for instance, is not remembered for the many failed attempts that he made but for the one that worked. Up until that point you could still have considered him a failure! Likewise, a sporting star is not judged by his or her unseen practice attempts, nor for that matter by scoring attempts on the way to stardom. If you look carefully at the record books you'll see that most scorers in games make many more failed attempts than successful ones. Overall, though, they make *more attempts* and that's why they do better than those of equal talent who do not expose themselves to the chance of failure quite so often.

Excuses for Not Writing

Despair brings with it strange bedfellows. Amongst those that will crawl into your mind in the midst of constant rejection are those ever popular excuses for not writing, for jacking it all in. Some of these you may be familiar with, some you may suffer from like an infection during your career, but you must be able to recognise them for what they are - excuses. Excuses that you make to yourself because you don't like getting rejected.

"I'm too ignorant or stupid to write" is a common complaint heard from the despairing. Chuck this thought into the bin for the rubbish that it is. If you're capable of reading this book then you are capable of writing one as good, if not better! There are plenty of people cleverer than you who will never get published, and plenty of people dimmer than you who will. Getting published is all about making a sale, in case you could have forgotten. You don't need the brain of a genius to be a published author. There's no law that makes you use big words - in fact, sesquipedalianism can be a negative trait rather than a positive one (see what I mean?). And even an inability to spell is no excuse these days; you can get a computer or typewriter to do the checking for you.

"I'm too busy to write" is another familiar song that you'll have sung in lots of other walks of life. In this context, can't means won't. Are you really saying that if, instead of rejections, scores of letters heaping praise on our work had arrived, you wouldn't have had the time to finish your product off? Or are you saying that because it's a good escape route from more possible rejections?

"I can't find time at the moment" is a variation on the above theme. When are you going to find time to carry out simple things like a mail shot or a few pages? Maybe your postponement is just a soft option, a lie that you can tell yourself. After a while, you'll come to believe it, and that will be that. Strange, though, how you've still got time to go out, watch television or read. But then again, those forms of activity don't run the risk of anyone mean and nasty saying no to you.

"I can't write because I haven't the inspiration." The answers to this one should all come in Anglo-Saxon, of the kind they didn't used to print! It's just an excuse, though a more poetic one than the others. Even if the Muse is sat firmly up her tree and can't be tempted with pleas or birdseed, there are still plenty of things that you can be doing to progress your work. You can send out tantalisers, chase up no-reply publishers and generally keep on top of your business - if you really want to, that is.

Vanity Unfair

Despair, an emotion that by now you are perhaps familiar with, is often named as a sin. So too is vanity. They come together in that species of publishing known as "vanity publishing" in which you, the author, pay a company to agree to publish your work. Like all sins it is best avoided, though in the midst of constant rejection it can seem tempting. Resist it. It is true that some famous authors made the big time after paying for publication, but there are a lot, lot more who have ended up with a badly-produced book that nobody would ever want to buy.

It may be necessary at the outset of your career to let your product go cheap, possibly even give samples away, but you are still a million miles away from vanity publishing. Vanity publishing can cost large amounts of money for mediocre results; no reviewer will touch your material, there is no distributor to help you shift your product, and no rep to get your books ordered by the bookshops. You may, perhaps, be one of those rare exceptions to that rule, but in the end it's best not to find out. Ignore the siren song of such "publishers" that are to be found in the papers every week. Concentrate instead of developing and then selling your product.

Diagnostics

Rather than giving up or falling prey to a vanity publisher, do something about your product-related problems. Go back to your hotel or quiet place with your year planner. Things will be much the same as they were the first time around with one major exception. This time you are not inventing a machine, you are fixing it. The parts are broken and disassembled, but it *will* work if only you follow the step-by-step instructions provided. Think back to the last occasion you put together some flat pack furniture or a childhood model kit, and remember how easy it was when you went by the correct sequence. Getting published is no different.

Begin, as they say, at the beginning. The single most common cause of despair (and subsequent failure) amongst salespeople of any sort is the lack of active prospecting. Unless enough initial contacts are made with prospects, no sale is going to happen. Do your records prove that you have contacted sufficient prospects to achieve a result? Have you contacted each prospect at least twice and alternated your activity between a variety of projects? Sometimes, when you get nothing but rejections, you can feel as if you have made a tremendous amount of contacts when in actual fact you haven't. Your sales log ought to provide hard figures; if they don't, or they are nonexistent, then you have the answer to your problem. Draw up a list of contacts, a programme of activity and *stick to it*.

Having first checked out the quantity of your sales work, now take a look at the quality. If you have indeed sent out tantalisers in the necessary numbers on a variety of projects and you haven't got through to the next level of the game, then something may be wrong with them. Tear up your originals and start all over again. Try to be more focused, sharper and businesslike in your efforts. Can you change your window dressing, offer a "new, improved formula" that will excite your prospects? Are there new buzzwords associated with your topic that can bring the sweet music of ringing cash tills to your prospect's finely-tuned ear? Experiment, draft and redraft until you get it right. This really is a vital piece of kit, so spend as much time and energy as required to make it work. Try getting a friend with no interest in that particular topic to read it and see if it piques their curiosity.

The same goes for your synopsis and sales proposal.

Examine every aspect of these crucial documents from length to the paper used. Is your layout reader-friendly, and is your case set out in a logical manner? Have you included a sufficient number of cash-suggestive phrases that make it easy to say "Yes"? Don't forget that these are sales documents, and you don't want your reader bogged down with details. You must take your reader to a mountain top where he or she can see the Promised Land overflowing with milk and money.

Moving on to the subject of your sample chapter, is it the right one? Have you succumbed to "First Chapteritis" and failed to get into the thick of things? Is it sufficiently loaded (see Jute) to get your prospect wanting more? If it isn't, write one that is.

Your problem may lay deeper than in mere presentation, however. It might be necessary to widen the scope of your product so that it appeals to a more general market, or to go in the opposite direction and make it seriously specialised. Similarly, you might have to consider going up- or downmarket in order to find a buyer. Consider the humble pen. A pen is a pen is a pen you might say, but there are many different kinds of pen. Some can be bought for a few pence whereas others can cost tens, hundreds and even thousands of pounds. There's no point whatsoever in trying to sell an expensive pen to a prospect who wants a cheap pen, nor a cheap pen to a prospect who lusts after an expensive one. Give the prospect what he or she wants, not what you want to sell!

The above measures, if followed conscientiously, ought to be sufficient to get you back on course. After a long spell of rejections, however, it's sometimes hard to break out of the depression that has settled over your efforts like a weather front. To rekindle your enthusiasm, try approaching your task from the alternative standpoints discussed below. Be like the tennis player who attacks their serve over and over again with a variety of different techniques until he or she gets it just right - experiment.

Writer's Circles
A simple, low-cost option you can take is to join a writer's circle. Most cities and towns now have such groups - check with your local library. (If there isn't one, then consider starting one up as part of your revised action plan.)

Although writing is to a large extent a solitary occupation, it can be useful to mix with other authors in search of a publisher. There are both emotional and practical benefits to be had by doing this. First and foremost, it will help reassure you that you are not alone, that rejection is quite a normal thing for an author to experience. Then again, the social bonds that you form will encourage activity. If you've said you'll meet so and so next week to read part of your latest work, you'll probably have it ready in time. And if you like the other members of the group you'll feel more positive about writing in general.

On a practical level, you can seek constructive criticism of a sort that you would have to pay for from other sources, i.e. training schools, agents. You should welcome rather than fear suggestions as to how your product can be improved - everybody else is in the same boat, so return the compliment. Nor should you be ashamed of such help, or feel that it somehow makes you less of an author. Quite a few well known books have been improved by informal "committees".

Reading your work aloud can also be of great value. You'll see things in the material that you hadn't noticed before, and the physical act will ready you for other sorts of public speaking.

Some writer's circles also function as publishing organisations. There may be a magazine or even a book of collected material to which you can contribute. Volumes of the latter sort can attract grants to subsidise publication, and allow you to kill two birds with one stone - you can see your material in print and use this to bolster your CV when presenting to a mainstream publisher.

From your hardened sales point of view, you can also encourage the circle to become a sort of "swop meet." Swop meet is an Americanism for a meeting between business people who are involved in related fields. An insurance agent, for instance, might share the same client base with a car salesperson, a garage, a builder and so on; the reverse is also true. The idea of a swop meet is to exchange hot leads on who is buying what for mutual profit. In literary terms, the publishers who have rejected you for a specific reason (i.e. too many pictures, too specialised) might be good for someone else. They too, might have just the right contact for you to exploit.

Networking

Networking is a modern term for an age-old business activity best summed up by an age-old saying which is "It's not what you know, it's who you know." Like most age-old sayings, it contains a fair amount of truth. Business transactions are carried out, as often as not, on the basis of personal contacts. Price, material, suitability, all of these factors and more are involved in the decision-making process, but a word in the right ear can overrule the lot. Getting published, as always, follows the same rules as any other business.

Put yourself, for a moment, in the position of an editor, director or producer. Every day there will be things that you want to do, things that you don't want to do, things you must do and a phone that never stops ringing. On top of everything else, there's a pile of something called new submissions. Submit is what you'll feel like doing when you see them lurking around your office. You know from experience that most of them will be rubbish, and the few that are hopeful will involve a disproportionate amount of time invested to money earned, unless one of them is an absolute bombshell you are probably going to send out a standard rejection letter and leave it at that.

Now suppose that sometime during that very same crowded day, you get an excited phone call from a person you like or have done profitable business with in the past. This person, who is actually nice to you, goes on to say that he or she has read this terrific proposal or met this terrific author that you'll love to bits. You could be a complete churl, of course, and snub your friend's effort to help you, but are you going to? Isn't your pal or business colleague worth a few minutes in your business schedule? With a sigh, you'll reach for the diary...

That's all there is to networking really. It's what agents do for a living; the only difference being that they (should) do it better and earn some money in the process. A DIY approach is harder, but it offers the same sort of rewards. Once inside the charmed circle of decision-makers, all things are possible. The only problem is getting inside in the first place.

The mechanisms used to reach key decision makers are essentially the same as those in looking for a coauthor as described in an earlier chapter. List everyone that you know who might possibly know someone useful or have contact with the kind of organisation that you are seeking to penetrate. You'll need to paint word pictures of the sort of person that you are seeking - those who work in TV, theatre, radio, other authors even.

With your list complete, you can start trawling. You need to meet with the most promising of your contacts with a view to them getting you in front of someone else. Get to be seen and heard in the right places where chance encounters with such individuals can become a reality. When you meet with them, don't fawn, beg or press your work upon them. Enthuse about your *topic*, not your product or yourself. (The latter must, in actual fact, be given a soft-sell.) Your love and knowledge of the subject must be your main attraction; the fact that you write is almost incidental. Mention your agent, however, whether or not you have one, just to guard against poaching.

Networking like this isn't easy, of course. It may take several, or many attempts to get where you want to be, but it's worth it in the end.

Call in the Plumber

Sometimes even household problems are beyond the scope of the average handyperson. Sometimes problems can require specialised knowledge and tools to put them right. In such circumstances, you would have no hesitation about calling in and paying someone with the necessary expertise. Nor should you when it comes to your writing. If the blockages that beset you are outside your capability to fix at the moment don't despair, call in the plumber!

Technical problems - for instance, difficulties with plotting, characterisation and so forth - can be resolved in a number of ways. Creative writing courses are now widely available at many colleges, and these might be all you need to give yourself a kick-start. More expensive, but more job-specific, are the sort of workshops advertised in literary or trade magazines. These are inevitably conducted by someone with real industry knowledge rather than just a scholastic approach. Yet another option is to sign on for correspondence courses in writing often seen in papers and magazines. These can help with technique but will not, repeat *will not*, guarantee publication. Only correct sales activity can guarantee that.

Another chargeable sort of advice comes from a number of agents or publishers. For a reading fee such companies will go through your manuscript and offer comments or a report. As might be expected, the quality of these can vary tremendously and often a friend could do just as well. Publishers, especially, who offer this service are best avoided - at least until they start offering to pay for the time spent writing the material in question.

The other area that you should perhaps consider seeking help with is in the repair of damage to yourself. Sustained rejection can damage ego and motivation to such an extent that DIY measures are not enough to do the job. In these circumstances you may wish to consult a performance coach or personal trainer. This may strike you as an odd notion, but in how many other occupations, hobbies or sports does the individual try to do it all alone? A performance coach can help you rediscover your enthusiasm, identify specific targets and help you shape new work patterns. Writing was likened earlier to a boxing match in which the author should expect to get hit hard and often. Look in the corner of any world champion and you'll see a coach cheering on.

Telephone Lines

Desperate situations call for equally desperate remedies. If, after putting all of the above into operation, you still haven't got the scent of success, then it's time to try something even more radical.

The fact that authors want to sell written books or scripts tends to blind them to the glaringly obvious, that what can be printed on a page can also be read aloud. A proposal does not have to be sold on paper; it can be sold over the phone.

Selling over the phone is now an established fact of business life. Count the times each day that you get such sales calls and multiply that by the millions of others worldwide. In "telesales", as it is usually known, a prospect is contacted on either a cold or referred basis. After some initial ice-breaking, he or she is then asked by the salesperson to agree to a physical meeting or is invited to make a purchase. It's as simple, and as hard, as that.

Telesales has a lot going for it. By using the phone, you can contact a lot of prospects in a very short space of time. Simultaneously, you can also weed out no-sale prospects and home in on the ones that are buying. You can duck and weave too, in a way that no tantaliser letter ever allows. If your prospect says that he or she wants it bigger or smaller, duller or brighter, you can retrace your steps and say that's what you had in mind all along.

So why doesn't every author sell over the phone? First and foremost, authors shy away from this activity because the concept of *selling* is still alien to them. They naively believe that people will buy on quality or need without further help and elaboration. Then again, it takes quite a degree of nerve or a degree of insanity just to ring someone up cold and say "Buy me, I'm the next..." A phone-wielding author faces practical problems too. Getting to actual decision-makers can be murder and the risks of rejection are high. And you won't sell your work there and then either. The best that can happen is that someone will say "OK, send me a chapter." But that's just want you want at this stage anyway, isn't it?

Telesales are considerably more involved a matter than picking up the phone and asking a prospect whether he or she wants to buy or not - do that, and you'll swiftly be disillusioned. Selling over the phone is an art in itself. In a very real sense, the sale begins before anything much is said at all. Your prospect has nothing to judge you by but the sound of your voice - there are no smiles, redeeming dimples or anything of that sort. Just a voice. Dead. How your prospect responds depends as much on the way you say it as what you say. Your prospect will like you or dismiss you within seconds, just as you might do to someone you've met at a party. Because of that, the first thing you must learn to do is smile down the phone. Smiling will alter the tone of your voice and relax the person on the other end of the phone. Try it out and see what happens. So important is this principle that the first thing telesales trainees are asked to do is bring a mirror to the office. Don't laugh - smile!

The sound of your voice also helps dictate the response that you receive. If you come across as calm, natural and unhurried, there is less chance that your prospect will blow you out cold. Think of how you respond to people who you assume to be "over" you, or of higher social standing. Or again, think of that big, tough-looking person in the pub and how you are going to talk to him or her. Nobody is dismissive of someone they are uncertain of. Don't give yourself the chance to be dismissed.

Other than a thick skin, the only further requirement for a telesales is a script. This may come as a shock, but you cannot afford to be unrehearsed and defenceless. You must have an answer ready for every single one of your prospect's objections. If you have to think about your replies then you'll lose. Your response to an objection has to be as swift and as sure as a tennis stroke. A script will also stop you rambling and allow you to identify your key selling points. You're a writer - write yourself a phone script!

Using the phone correctly can help you find a publisher or an agent. Before you attempt this course of action, however, make sure that you know what you are doing: the books by Schiffman and Hopkins (see Appendix; Further Reading) tell you all you need to know.

Face Fax

Modern technology offers you other methods of getting to your prospect. The faxed message is the easiest and cheapest of these. If you decide to pursue this option ensure that (a) your fax arrives on a day when your topic is hot news, and (b) that it is short. The aim is to excite and tantalise - risk saying too little rather than too much. Make your prospect come to you.

Got it Taped?

You can also try sending your prospect a taped introduction to your product that he or she can listen to it on the way into work. Feed your prospect's self-image and power trip with an acknowledgement of their "hectic" lifestyle: he or she is so busy, but that this really is the *only* way a few seconds can be spared.

Keep your message short and simple. If you feel bad about the sound of your voice, get someone else to record for you. Worry about the ethics later; for now just sell.

Evolution

Not every strategy that you try is going to work every time, and even the cutest trick will get spotted for what it is in the end. Despite what you may think, publishers are not unintelligent, and they don't like being sold to any more than any other prospect. The secret rests in making the sale invisible, making it appear that the decision to buy was wholly the prospect's.

Take another lesson from Nature, that of the constancy

of evolution. It might start with a tasty plant developing spines. Along comes an animal with spine-crushing teeth, whereupon the plant develops poisons. Lo and behold, along comes an animal that just can't get enough of plant poisons. And so it goes, on and on and on...

The struggle between prospect and salesperson is every bit as constant and mutable as the one described above. Don't get trapped into thinking in straight lines in your efforts to get published. Be prepared to adapt, invent and test sales methods that work for you. Evolve.

Chapter Nine

<u>Beyond Failure</u>

It took me fifteen years to discover that I had no talent for writing, but I couldn't give it up because by that time I was too famous.
Robert Benchley

It takes twenty years to make an overnight success.
Eddie Canter

I'm a great believer in luck, and I find the harder I work the more I have of it.
Thomas Jefferson

Good Buys

You do not have to be a great author to get published
or produced - you don't even have to be a good one!
All that is required is that you understand and utilise
the principles of buying and selling to their fullest
extent. If you do that, and work hard enough, success
is inevitable because of another important rule of
business, which is:

Prospects love to say yes.

Prospects really, truly *do* want to buy. They want to
make that purchase because doing so will make they
feel strong and in control of their lives. They want to
buy that product because it will make them feel special.
They want to say "Yes" to that salesperson because
making him or her happy will also make them feel happy
inside.

   Publishers are just like anyone else when it comes to
buying. Like any other prospect, their desire to purchase
is troubled by "static" - worries about cost, suitability
and need. Your job as a salesperson is to remove those
obstacles to making a positive decision.

The End of the Beginning
Three principles to live and work by:

Failure is possible only when I stop trying.
Until such time as you vow never to write again and
mean it, you cannot take the easy option and gloat over
the "fact" that you are a failure. No matter how many
rejections you receive, no matter how many
disappointments you suffer, so long as you are writing
you are working towards your goal. So it's painful, so it
takes a while, so what? Calling yourself a failure or no
good is just a cop out. You're really saying that you are
either too vain or too lazy to make the changes in your
operational style that will lead to success. Make those
changes and you will almost certainly sell something to
somebody. Now *that's* a fact.

Success is what I say it is.
Just as failure is defined in personal terms, so is success.
You and you alone ultimately decide you have set what
success is, and if you have set precise, realistic,
achievable, measurable, and understood goals, then you
are already halfway there. Don't lay impossible burdens
on yourself, or castigate yourself for not being a Bronte,
a Conrad or a Marlowe. Do the best you can with what
you've got and achieve publication. That's the first and
most important goal, isn't it?

Somewhere, somehow, someone will buy what I have to offer in some shape or form.

Everything is down to numbers and if you don't allow rejections to blind you to that central truth, you will get published. It may not take the form that you envisage right now (your comedy might turn into a tragedy, your textbook into an idiot's guide and so on) but it *is* going to happen if you let it. Remember, people *want* to buy. You just have to make it easy for them to say yes.

An Anonymous Message

Overcoming rejection by publishers is largely a matter of persistence and activity. In most cases the authors who fail - that is, do not get published - fail because they misunderstand the facts of life. Getting published is not about talent or worth but about selling a product. You are involved in a business transaction, not a literary competition, and you must keep always keep that fact in front of you. Pay attention to the business side of things and the writing will look after itself.

Sales people are very fond of uplifting stories and poems enshrining certain sacred principles. One that is widely heard in the sales environment is by the great poet Anon, who really should have paid more attention to the business side of writing. (He or she would have made a fortune in royalties!) Put this poem in your computer, over your typewriter or learn it by heart.

Make it the first practical step you take in your new found career as a salesperson and then get ready for success.

Don't Quit
When things go wrong, as they often will,
When the road you're walking seems all up hill,
When funds are low and debts are high,
And you want to smile but have to sigh,
When care is pressing down a bit,
Rest if you must, but don't you quit.

Life is queer with twists and turns,
As everyone of us sometimes learns;
And many a fellow turns about,
When he might have won if he'd stuck it out.
Don't give up though things seem slow,
You might succeed with another blow.

Oft the goal is nearer than it seems
To a faint and faltering man;
Often the struggle is given up,
When he might have captured the victor's cup,
And he learned too late when night came down,
How close he was to the golden crown.

Success is failure turned inside out,
The silver tint of the clouds of doubt,
And you never can tell how close you are,
It may be near when it seems afar.
So stick to the fight when you're hardest hit:
It's when things seem worse that you mustn't quit.

Anon

Envoi: Don't get sad, get published.

Appendix

Recommended Reading

Listed below, in no particular order of merit or preference, is a selection of books that you will find invaluable in your career of Author-As-Salesperson. Read, and then apply the advice that they contain; your goal, remember, is to sell your product to a prospect who just happens to be called a publisher. At the end of the day your skill in self-promotion is just as important as any literary talent that you might or might not possess.

Writing Proposals and Synopses That Sell
Andre Jute, Thames & Lochar (1994)
ISBN 0 946537 96 8

Do whatever it takes to get hold of this book. Jute's treatment of this phase of the sale is both definitive and readable. Essential.

Dare to be a Great Writer
Leonard Bishop, Writer's Digest Books (1988)
ISBN 0 89879 464 1

Slightly evangelical in tone, and at times sounding like the script for the next "Rocky" outing, this is nonetheless a work of great merit. Although most of the advice offered is directed towards writing rather than selling, what sales tips it does offer are dynamite. Well worth your time.

How to Master the Art of Selling
Tom Hopkins, Collins (1983)
ISBN 0 586 05896 6

Hopkins' book is so good that it almost removes the need for any other, including this one! As the blurb states, it is the best ever written on the subject of selling. Utterly, utterly brilliant.

Unlimited Power
Anthony Robbins, Simon & Schuster (1988)
ISBN 0 671 65445

The Mother of all self-development texts. Full of psychological insights that will serve you both in the realm of rejections and the dizzying heights of the publisher's office. Very, very useful.

How to Make Money Scriptwriting
Julian Friedman, Boxtree (1995)

As its title suggests, Friedman's "guerilla guide to selling" leans towards film and TV writing. Authors of any sort, however, will find much of interest in this very professional work by a very professional agent.

Wealth 101: Getting What You Want, Enjoying What You've Got
John Roger and Peter McWilliams, Thorsons (1992)
ISBN 07225 28558

The road you have chosen for yourself is going to hurt, make no mistake about it. You're going to get hit hard and often, and if you want to survive you'll need to roll with the punches. Self-help books, of which this is one of the very best, make excellent sticking plasters for the bruised ego. A work to be read and treasured, not least for its repository of quotes and observations.

Live the Life You Love
Barbara Sher, Hodder & Stoughton (1996)
ISBN 07336 0386 6

Another excellent self-help text that is packed solid with useful ideas and techniques. Sher's "ten easy lessons" approach to the attaining of goals might turn some on and some off. If you fall into the first category read it; if into the second, read it anyway.

Power Selling
Michael Friedman and Jeffrey Weiss, Thorsons (1989)
ISBN 0 7225 1922 2

Sometimes you can pick up a really thick book and "feel" that it's going to be a really good buy. This is one of them. If you only take in a small percentage of the sales psychology on offer here you will come away far, far richer.

Adventures in the Screen Trade: A Personal View of Hollywood
William Goldman, Abacus (1996)
ISBN 0 349 1075 X

A must for anyone wanting to write films! Although this book is concerned mainly with the American scene, its general principles hold true in any movie environment. One to read for pleasure as well as profitable instruction.

The Essential Ellison
Terry Dowling (ed.), Morpeus (1993)

Harlan Ellison is one of the greatest short story writers that America, or for that matter, the world, has ever seen. He is also the survivor of myriad battles with publishing houses and producers who tried to draw the venom from his fangs. If "My Way" is your theme song, and Art means all, make this guy your patron saint. "Somehow, I Don't Think We're in Kansas, Toto" will prepare you for war; "Driving In The Spikes" will show you what to do if you lose it.

Cold Calling Techniques That Really Work
Steven Schiffman, Kogan Page (1988)

If you intend to broaden your sales opportunities by use of the telephone, then this is the master work to consult. Direct, clever and practical, it offers everything that you need to sell yourself down the wires.

Creative Thinking: How to Generate Ideas and then Turn Them into Successful Reality
Michael Le Boeuf, Piatkus (1994)
ISBN 0 7499 1633 8

Creative thinking is essential to you in both your writing and your selling work. The writing bit may be obvious to you, the selling less so. As a salesperson you need to be developing new strategies, new angles. Prospects develop resistance to sales techniques just like germs develop resistance to antibiotics, so beat their immune system by changing. This feel-good factor-ten book is an excellent guide to this process. Read it.

Body Language: How to Read Other's Thoughts by Their Gestures
Allan Pease, Sheldon Press (1991)
ISBN 0 85969 406 2

This is the best general introduction to the subject of body language available. Full of diagrams and notes, it will equip you splendidly for face to face encounters with prospects of every sort. Useful, too, if you're writing fiction or television and film. Highly recommended.

BESTSELLERS

TOP WRITERS TELL HOW

Richard Joseph

Richard Joseph interviews 23 of the world's most famous authors to find out just what made their books bestsellers. Readers can learn where Barbara Cartland gets her inspiration, discover what gave former jockey Dick Francis the confidence to write about horses instead of just training them and why Tom Clancy set alarm bells ringing in the Pentagon.

Richard Joseph's incisive and entertaining interviews will appeal to all fans of such best-selling authors as Frederick Forsyth, Robert Ludlum, Joseph Wambaugh, James Michener, Arthur Hailey and more. Perhaps aspiring writers will discover the secret to their success — and discover their own.

". . . the best shot at spelling out to would-be writers what it takes to make the grade"
The Times

BESTSELLERS

TOP WRITERS TELL HOW
Richard Joseph
288 pages, Hardback,
UK £15.99, USA $25.95, CAN $34.99
ISBN 1-84024-009-1
SUMMERSDALE

RICHARD JOSEPH'S

BESTSELLERS

TOP WRITERS
TELL
HOW

JEFFREY ARCHER   DICK FRANCIS   CLIVE CUSSLER
BARBARA TAYLOR BRADFORD   JILLY COOPER
CATHERINE COOKSON   TOM CLANCY   FREDERICK FORSYTH
and many more

SUMMERSDALE